**adds value to business,
work and life.**

Employers are responsible for providing a safe and healthy workplace for their employees. OSHA's role is to promote the safety and health of America's working men and women by setting and enforcing standards; providing training, outreach and education; establishing partnerships; and encouraging continual improvement in workplace safety and health.

This publication provides a general overview of a particular standards-related topic. This publication does not alter or determine compliance responsibilities which are set forth in OSHA standards, and the *Occupational Safety and Health Act*. Moreover, because interpretations and enforcement policy may change over time, for additional guidance on OSHA compliance requirements the reader should consult current administrative interpretations and decisions by the Occupational Safety and Health Review Commission and the courts.

Material contained in this publication is in the public domain and may be reproduced, fully or partially, without permission. Source credit is requested but not required.

This information will be made available to sensory impaired individuals upon request. Voice phone: (202) 693-1999; teletypewriter (TTY) number: 1-877-889-5627.

Assigned Protection Factors
for the
Revised Respiratory Protection Standard

**Occupational Safety and Health Administration
U.S. Department of Labor**

OSHA 3352-02
2009

Original cover Illustrations created by Attiliis & Associates

Contents

Introduction

In a final rule on Assigned Protection Factors (APFs), OSHA revised its existing Respiratory Protection standard to add definitions and requirements for APFs and Maximum Use Concentrations (MUCs). (See 63 FR 1152; 29 CFR 1910.134; 71 FR 50122, August 24, 2006.) This guidance document focuses on the mandatory selection provisions of the APFs, MUCs, and Table I [1] at page 14 and their role in the overall Respiratory Protection standard. The provisions can only be used when respirators are properly selected and used in compliance with the full Respiratory Protection standard. The final Respiratory Protection standard (29 CFR 1910.134 and 29 CFR 1926.103) applies to general industry, construction, longshoring, shipyard, and marine terminal workplaces.

The Agency developed the final APFs after thoroughly reviewing the available literature, including workplace protection factor studies, comments submitted to the record, and hearing testimony. The final APFs provide employers with critical information to use when selecting respirators for employees exposed to atmospheric contaminants found in industry. Proper respirator selection is an important component of an effective respiratory protection program. Accordingly, the final APFs are necessary to protect employees who must use respirators to protect them from airborne contaminants.

The Audience for this Guide

The employer should read this guide if it is likely that you will need to establish and implement a respiratory protection program.

How to Use this Guide

This guide is divided into sections that correspond to the recently updated respirator selection provisions under section (d) of the Respiratory Protection standard. Specifically, these provisions are (d)(3)(i)(A) and (d)(3)(i)(B). This guide provides information that answers the following questions: What are Assigned Protection Factors (APFs)?; What are Maximum Use Concentrations (MUCs)?; and How to Use APFs and MUCs?

Two attachments are provided. Attachment A is the glossary of the final APF rule; and, Attachment B is the complete final Respiratory Protection standard. The brown colored type denotes that the provisions of the final Respiratory Protection standard are being used.

History

In a final rule on OSHA's Respiratory Protection standard, OSHA reserved the provisions incorporating APFs, MUCs, and the APF Table, for further rulemaking. (See 63 FR 1152; 29 CFR 1910.134; 71 FR 50122, August 24, 2006.) The APF final standard went into effect on November 22, 2006 (71 FR 50122).

OSHA's methodology for assigning protection factors to classes of respirators was twofold: first, OSHA analyzed all the data, and second, OSHA reviewed all the literature. By analyzing all available statistical data and literature, OSHA is assured that the Agency is measuring and observing the outcomes that are of concern to OSHA. That is, OSHA is observing and measuring the outcomes achieved when employers are in compliance with the full Respiratory Protection standard. Thus, OSHA has acted in a rigorous manner in establishing the APFs.

Assigned Protection Factors (APFs) and Maximum Use Concentrations (MUCs)

The rulemaking on the reserved sections of the Respiratory Protection standard have now been completed (71 FR 50122; August 24, 2006). These cover provisions for APFs and MUCs, as well as Table I.

The definitions of APFs and MUCs are:

Assigned Protection Factor (APF) means the workplace level of respiratory protection that a respirator or class of respirators is expected to provide to employees when the employer implements a continuing, effective respiratory protection program as specified by this section.

Maximum Use Concentration (MUC) means the maximum atmospheric concentration of a hazardous substance from which an employee can be expected to be protected when wearing a respirator, and is determined by the assigned protection factor of the respirator or class of respirators and the exposure limit of the hazardous substance. The MUC usually can be determined mathematically by multiplying the assigned protection factor specified for a respirator by the permissible exposure limit (PEL), short-term exposure limit, ceiling limit, peak limit, or any other exposure limit used for the hazardous substance.

The MUC for respirators is calculated by multiplying the APF for the respirator by the PEL. The MUC is the upper limit at which the class of respirator is expected to provide protection. Whenever the exposures approach the MUC, then the employer should select the next higher class of respirators for the employees.

Employers must not apply MUCs to conditions that are immediately dangerous to life or health (IDLH); instead, they must use respirators listed for IDLH conditions in paragraph (d)(2) of this standard. When the calculated MUC exceeds the IDLH level for a hazardous substance, or the performance limits of the cartridge or canister, then employers must set the maximum MUC at that lower limit.

How to use APFs and MUCs

Under the Respiratory Protection standard, APFs and MUCs are used specifically in selecting proper equipment under section (d)(3), which addresses the selection of respiratory protection equipment for non-IDLH atmospheres. In this provision, under (d)(3)(i), employers must provide respirators that are adequate to protect employee health and ensure compliance with all other OSHA requirements under routine, and reasonably foreseeable, emergency situations.

Under paragraph (d)(3)(i)(A), employers must select respirators according to APFs, using Table I: Assigned Protection Factors. Under paragraph (d)(3)(i)(B), employers must select respirators after considering the MUCs in their workplace under which respirators are to be used.

APFs are used to select the appropriate class of respirators that will provide the necessary level of protection. The airborne hazardous exposure can be from a particulate or a gas or vapor. The APF for the class of respirators will remain the same. The APF value can only be applied to a class of respirators when the respirators are properly selected and used in compliance with the Respiratory Protection standard (29 CFR 1910.134), with properly selected filters or canisters, as needed.

The new APF table is on page 14.

Under paragraph (d)(3)(ii), employers must select respirators (using APFs as well) that are appropriate for the chemical state and physical form of the contaminant. You need different types of filters, cartridges, and canisters depending on whether dusts, fumes, mists, vapors, or gases are present in your workplace and depending on the kinds and concentrations of the substances present.

Respiratory hazards may be present in the workplace whenever an atmosphere does not contain sufficient oxygen, or if it contains chemical, biological, or radiological contaminants in sufficient quantity to harm the health of employees. Respiratory hazards may be present in the workplace in the following physical forms:

Dusts and fibers are solid particles that are formed or generated from solid materials through mechanical processes such as crushing, grinding, drilling, abrading or blasting. Examples are lead, silica, and asbestos.

Fumes are solid particles that are formed when a metal or other solid vaporizes and the molecules condense (or solidify) in cool air. Examples are metal fumes from smelting or welding. Fumes also may be formed from processes such as plastic injection or extrusion molding.

Mists are tiny droplets of liquid suspended in the air. Examples are oil mist produced from lubricants used in metal cutting operations, acid mists from electroplating, and paint spray mist from spraying operations.

Gases are materials that exist as individual molecules in the air at room temperature. Examples are welding gases, such as acetylene and nitrogen, and carbon monoxide produced from internal combustion engines.

Vapors are the gaseous form of substances that are normally in the solid or liquid state at room temperature and pressure. They are formed by evaporation. Most solvents produce vapors. Examples include toluene and methylene chloride.

Biological hazards include bacteria, viruses, fungi, and other living organisms that are respirable and can cause acute and chronic infections. Examples include Legionnaire's Disease and animal waste products (e.g., feces).

www.osha.gov

Occupational Safety and
Health Administration

Major Types of Respirators

Air-purifying respirators, which remove contaminants from the air.

Half mask/Dust mask
APF=10
Needs to be fit tested

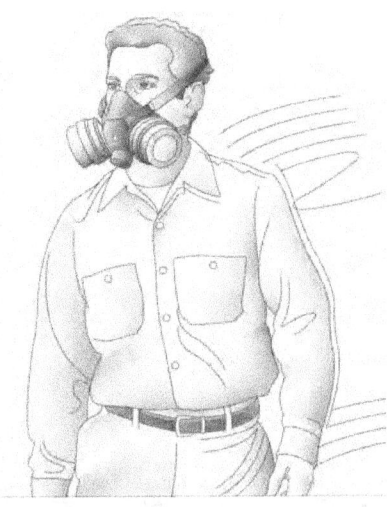

Half mask (Elastomeric)
APF=10
Needs to be fit tested

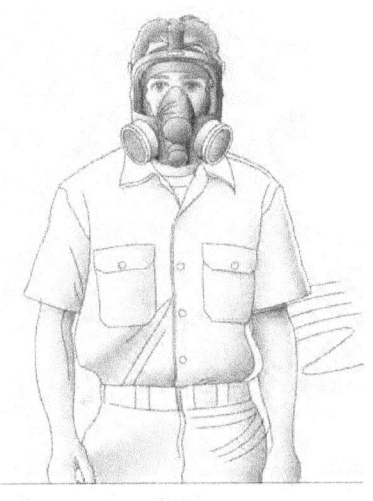

Full facepiece (Elastomeric)
APF=50
Needs to be fit tested

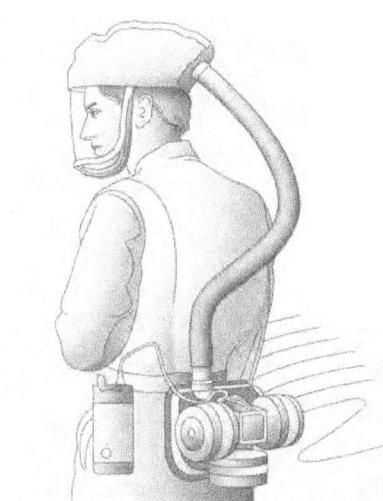

**Loose-Fitting Powered
Air-Purifying Respirator (PAPR)**
APF= 25

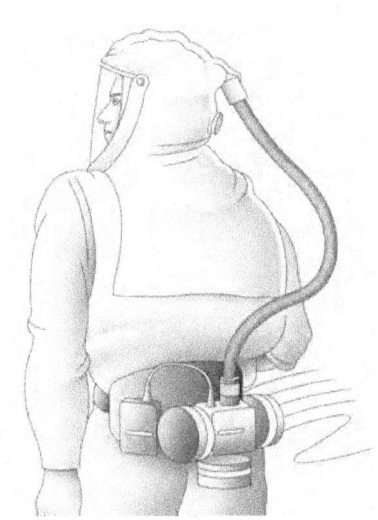

**Hood Powered Air-Purifying
Respirator (PAPR)**
APF= 25

Atmosphere-supplying respirators, which provide clean air from an uncontaminated source.

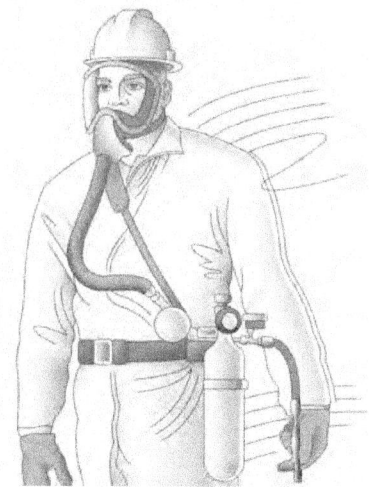

Full Facepiece Supplied-Air Respirator (SAR) with an auxiliary Escape Bottle
APF=1,000
APF = 10,000 (if used in "escape" mode)
Needs to be fit tested

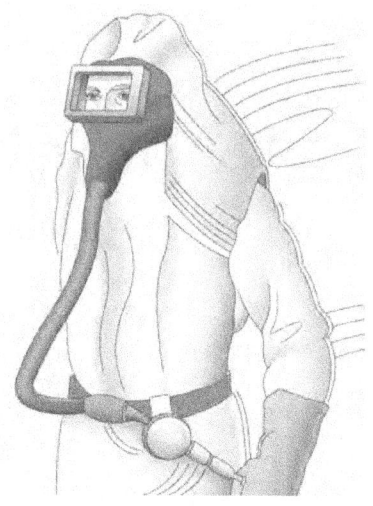

Full Facepiece Abrasive Blasting Continuous Flow
APF=1,000
Needs to be fit tested

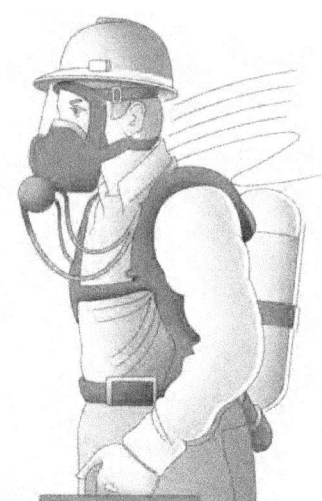

Full Facepiece Self-Contained Breathing Apparatus (SCBA)
Pressure demand mode is APF=10,000
Needs to be fit tested

OSHA®
www.osha.gov
Occupational Safety and Health Administration

Attachment A
Glossary

At the beginning of the final rule for Assigned Protection Factors (APF), in a separate glossary, there are lists for both acronyms and common terms used throughout the preamble to the final APF rule. (See 63 FR 1152; 29 CFR 1910.134; 71 FR 50122, August 24, 2006). The glossary is provided as an auxiliary list for terms used both in the APF rulemaking as well as throughout the preamble to the APF final rule. This glossary is in addition to the definitions in the APF rulemaking for Assigned Protection Factor and Maximum Use Concentration (MUC). The glossary contains legally defined terms from the final Respiratory Protection standard (29 CFR 1910.134 and 29 CFR 1926.103) each of which is highlighted with an asterisk (*). The purpose of this glossary and list of acronyms is to provide the terms that have already been defined by the Respiratory Protection standard, in one place, along with the terms from the final APF rule in order to facilitate their use and review.

This glossary specifies the terms represented by acronyms and provides definitions of other terms used frequently in the preamble to the final rule. This glossary does not change the legal requirements in this final rule nor is it intended to impose new regulatory requirements on the regulated community.

Acronyms

ACGIH	American Conference of Governmental Industrial Hygienists
AIHA	American Industrial Hygiene Association
ANSI	American National Standards Institute
APF	Assigned Protection Factor
APR	Air-purifying respirator
C_i	Concentration measured inside the respirator facepiece
C_o	Concentration measured outside the respirator
DOP	Dioctylphthalate (see definition at page 8)
DFM	Dust, fume, and mist filter
EPF	Effective Protection Factor (see definition at page 9)
HEPA	High efficiency particulate air filter (see definition at page 8)
IDLH	Immediately dangerous to life or health (see definition at page 8, and under the Respiratory Protection standard)
LANL	Los Alamos National Laboratory
LASL	Los Alamos Scientific Laboratory
LLNL	Lawrence Livermore National Laboratory
MSHA	Mine Safety and Health Administration
MUC	Maximum Use Concentration
NFPA	National Fire Protection Association
NIOSH	National Institute for Occupational Safety and Health
NRC	Nuclear Regulatory Commission
OSHA	Occupational Safety and Health Administration
OSH Act	Occupational Safety and Health Act of 1970 (29 U.S.C. 655, 657, 665).
PAPR	Powered air-purifying respirator (see definition in the standard below)
PEL	Permissible Exposure Limit
PPF	Program Protection Factor (see definition at page 8)
QLFT	Qualitative fit test (see definition at page 9)
QNFT	Quantitative fit test (see definition at page 9)
RDL	Respirator Decision Logic (see definition at page 9)
REL	Recommended Exposure Limit (see definition at page 9)
SAR	Supplied-air (or airline) respirator (see definition at page 9)
SCBA	Self-contained breathing apparatus (see definition at page 9)
WPF	Workplace Protection Factor (see definition at page 9)
TLV	Threshold Limit Value (see definition at page 9)
SWPF	Simulated Workplace Protection Factor (see definition at page 9)

Definitions

Terms preceded by an asterisk (*) refer to definitions that can be found in paragraph (b) ("Definitions") of OSHA's Respiratory Protection standard (29 CFR 1910.134).

*Air-purifying respirator: A respirator with an air-purifying filter, cartridge, or canister that removes specific air contaminants by passing ambient air through the air-purifying element.

*Atmosphere-supplying respirator: A respirator that supplies the respirator user with breathing air from a source independent of the ambient atmosphere, and includes SARs and SCBA units.

*Canister or cartridge: A container with a filter, sorbent, or catalyst, or combination of these items, which removes specific contaminants from the air passed through the container.

Continuous flow respirator: An atmosphere-supplying respirator that provides a continuous flow of breathable air to the respirator facepiece.

*Demand respirator: An atmosphere-supplying respirator that admits breathing air to the facepiece only when a negative pressure is created inside the facepiece by inhalation.

Dioctylphthalate (DOP): An aerosolized agent used for quantitative fit testing.

Elastomeric: A respirator facepiece made of a natural or synthetic elastic material such as natural rubber, silicone, or EPDM rubber.

*Filter or air-purifying element: A component used in respirators to remove solid or liquid aerosols from the inspired air.

*Filtering facepiece (or dust mask): A negative pressure particulate respirator with a filter as an integral part of the facepiece or with the entire facepiece composed of the filtering medium.

*Fit factor: A quantitative estimate of the fit of a particular respirator to a specific individual, and typically estimates the ratio of the concentration of a substance in ambient air to its concentration inside the respirator when worn.

*Fit test: The use of a protocol to qualitatively or quantitatively evaluate the fit of a respirator on an individual.

*Helmet: A rigid respiratory inlet covering that also provides head protection against impact and penetration.

*High efficiency particulate air filter (HEPA): A filter that is at least 99.97% efficient in removing monodisperse particles of 0.3 micrometers in diameter. The equivalent NIOSH 42 CFR 84 particulate filters are the N100, R100, and P100 filters.

*Hood: A respiratory inlet covering that completely covers the head and neck and may also cover portions of the shoulders and torso.

*Immediately dangerous to life or health (IDLH): An atmosphere that poses an immediate threat to life, would cause irreversible adverse health effects, or would impair an individual's ability to escape from a dangerous atmosphere.

*Loose-fitting facepiece: A respiratory inlet covering that is designed to form a partial seal with the face.

*Negative pressure respirator (tight-fitting): A respirator in which the air pressure inside the facepiece is negative during inhalation with respect to the ambient air pressure outside the respirator.

Permissible Exposure Limit (PEL): An occupational exposure limit specified by OSHA.

*Positive pressure respirator: A respirator in which the pressure inside the respiratory inlet covering exceeds the ambient air pressure outside the respirator.

*Powered air-purifying respirator (PAPR): An air-purifying respirator that uses a blower to force the ambient air through air-purifying elements to the inlet covering.

*Pressure demand respirator: A positive pressure atmosphere-supplying respirator that admits breathing air to the facepiece when the positive pressure is reduced inside the facepiece by inhalation.

Protection factor study: A study that determines the protection provided by a respirator during use. This determination generally is accomplished by measuring the ratio of the concentration of an airborne contaminant (e.g., hazardous substance) outside the respirator (C_o) to the concentration inside the respirator (C_i) (i.e., C_o/C_i). Therefore, as the ratio between C_o and C_i increases, the protection factor increases, indicating an increase in the level of protection pro-

vided to employees by the respirator. Four types of protection factor studies are:

Effective Protection Factor (EPF) study - a study, conducted in the workplace, that measures the protection provided by a properly selected, fit tested, and functioning respirator when used intermittently for only some fraction of the total workplace exposure time (i.e., sampling is conducted during periods when respirators are worn and not worn). EPFs are not directly comparable to WPF values because the determinations include both the time spent in contaminated atmospheres with and without respiratory protection; therefore, EPFs usually underestimate the protection afforded by a respirator that is used continuously in the workplace.

Program Protection Factor (PPF) study - a study that estimates the protection provided by a respirator within a specific respirator program. Like the EPF, it is focused not only on the respirator's performance, but also the effectiveness of the complete respirator program. PPFs are affected by all factors of the program, including respirator selection and maintenance, user training and motivation, work activities, and program administration.

Workplace Protection Factor (WPF) study - a study, conducted under actual conditions of use in the workplace, that measures the protection provided by a properly selected, fit tested, and functioning respirator, when the respirator is worn correctly and used as part of a comprehensive respirator program that is in compliance with OSHA's Respiratory Protection standard at 29 CFR 1910.134. Measurements of Co and Ci are obtained only while the respirator is being worn during performance of normal work tasks (i.e., samples are not collected when the respirator is not being worn). As the degree of protection afforded by the respirator increases, the WPF increases.

Simulated Workplace Protection Factor (SWPF) study - a study, conducted in a controlled laboratory setting and in which Co and Ci sampling is performed while the respirator user performs a series of set exercises. The laboratory setting is used to control many of the variables found in workplace studies, while the exercises simulate the work activities of respirator users. This type of study is designed to determine the optimum performance of respirators by reducing the impact of sources of variability through maintenance of tightly controlled study conditions.

*Qualitative fit test (QLFT): A pass/fail fit test to assess the adequacy of respirator fit that relies on the individual's response to the test agent.

*Quantitative fit test (QNFT): An assessment of the adequacy of respirator fit by numerically measuring the amount of leakage into the respirator.

Recommended Exposure Limit (REL): An occupational exposure level recommended by NIOSH.

Respirator Decision Logic (RDL): Respirator selection guidance developed by NIOSH that contains a set of respirator protection factors.

*Self-contained breathing apparatus (SCBA): An atmosphere-supplying respirator for which the breathing air source is designed to be carried by the user.

*Supplied-air respirator (or airline) respirator (SAR): An atmosphere-supplying respirator for which the source of breathing air is not designed to be carried by the user.

Threshold Limit Value (TLV): An occupational exposure level recommended by ACGIH.

*Tight-fitting facepiece: A respiratory inlet covering that forms a complete seal with the face.

Attachment B
Regulatory Text of the Respiratory Protection Standard

For additional information about proper selection and use of respiratory protection, see the final Respiratory Protection standard (29 CFR 1910.134), below.

1910.134(a)
Permissible practice.

1910.134(a)(1)
In the control of those occupational diseases caused by breathing air contaminated with harmful dusts, fogs, fumes, mists, gases, smokes, sprays, or vapors, the primary objective shall be to prevent atmospheric contamination. This shall be accomplished as far as feasible by accepted engineering control measures (for example, enclosure or confinement of the operation, general and local ventilation, and substitution of less toxic materials). When effective engineering controls are not feasible, or while they are being instituted, appropriate respirators shall be used pursuant to this section.

1910.134(a)(2)
Respirators shall be provided by the employer when such equipment is necessary to protect the health of the employee. The employer shall provide the respirators which are applicable and suitable for the purpose intended. The employer shall be responsible for the establishment and maintenance of a respiratory protection program which shall include the requirements outlined in paragraph (c) of this section.

1910.134(b)
Definitions.
The following definitions are important terms used in the respiratory protection standard in this section.

Air-purifying respirator means a respirator with an air-purifying filter, cartridge, or canister that removes specific air contaminants by passing ambient air through the air-purifying element.

Assigned protection factor (APF) means the workplace level of respiratory protection that a respirator or class of respirators is expected to provide to employees when the employer implements a continuing, effective respiratory protection program as specified by this section.

Atmosphere-supplying respirator means a respirator that supplies the respirator user with breathing air from a source independent of the ambient atmosphere, and includes supplied-air respirators (SARs) and self-contained breathing apparatus (SCBA) units.

Canister or cartridge means a container with a filter, sorbent, or catalyst, or combination of these items, which removes specific contaminants from the air passed through the container.

Demand respirator means an atmosphere-supplying respirator that admits breathing air to the facepiece only when a negative pressure is created inside the facepiece by inhalation.

Emergency situation means any occurrence such as, but not limited to, equipment failure, rupture of containers, or failure of control equipment that may or does result in an uncontrolled significant release of an airborne contaminant.

Employee exposure means exposure to a concentration of an airborne contaminant that would occur if the employee were not using respiratory protection.

End-of-service-life indicator (ESLI) means a system that warns the respirator user of the approach of the end of adequate respiratory protection, for example, that the sorbent is approaching saturation or is no longer effective.

Escape-only respirator means a respirator intended to be used only for emergency exit.

Filter or air purifying element means a component used in respirators to remove solid or liquid aerosols from the inspired air.

Filtering facepiece (dust mask) means a negative pressure particulate respirator with a filter as an integral part of the facepiece or with the entire facepiece composed of the filtering medium.

Fit factor means a quantitative estimate of the fit of a particular respirator to a specific individual, and typically estimates the ratio of the concentration of a substance in ambient air to its concentration inside the respirator when worn.

Fit test means the use of a protocol to qualitatively or quantitatively evaluate the fit of a respirator on an individual. (See also Qualitative fit test QLFT and Quantitative fit test QNFT.)

Helmet means a rigid respiratory inlet covering that also provides head protection against impact and penetration.

High efficiency particulate air (HEPA) filter means a filter that is at least 99.97% efficient in removing monodisperse particles of 0.3 micrometers in diameter. The equivalent NIOSH 42 CFR 84 particulate filters are the N100, R100, and P100 filters.

Hood means a respiratory inlet covering that completely covers the head and neck and may also cover portions of the shoulders and torso.

Immediately dangerous to life or health (IDLH) means an atmosphere that poses an immediate threat to life, would cause irreversible adverse health effects, or would impair an individual's ability to escape from a dangerous atmosphere.

Interior structural firefighting means the physical activity of fire suppression, rescue or both, inside of buildings or enclosed structures which are involved in a fire situation beyond the incipient stage. (See 29 CFR 1910.155)

Loose-fitting facepiece means a respiratory inlet covering that is designed to form a partial seal with the face.

Maximum use concentration (MUC) means the maximum atmospheric concentration of a hazardous substance from which an employee can be expected to be protected when wearing a respirator, and is determined by the assigned protection factor of the respirator or class of respirators and the exposure limit of the hazardous substance. The MUC can be determined mathematically by multiplying the assigned protection factor specified for a respirator by the required OSHA permissible exposure limit, short-term exposure limit, or ceiling limit. When no OSHA exposure limit is available for a hazardous substance, an employer must determine an MUC on the basis of relevant available information and informed professional judgment.

Negative pressure respirator (tight fitting) means a respirator in which the air pressure inside the facepiece is negative during inhalation with respect to the ambient air pressure outside the respirator.

Oxygen deficient atmosphere means an atmosphere with an oxygen content below 19.5% by volume.

Physician or other licensed healthcare professional (PLHCP) means an individual whose legally permitted scope of practice (i.e., license, registration, or certification) allows him or her to independently provide, or be delegated the responsibility to provide, some or all of the healthcare services required by paragraph (e) of this section.

Positive pressure respirator means a respirator in which the pressure inside the respiratory inlet covering exceeds the ambient air pressure outside the respirator.

Powered air-purifying respirator (PAPR) means an air-purifying respirator that uses a blower to force the ambient air through air-purifying elements to the inlet covering.

Pressure demand respirator means a positive pressure atmosphere-supplying respirator that admits breathing air to the facepiece when the positive pressure is reduced inside the facepiece by inhalation.

Qualitative fit test (QLFT) means a pass/fail fit test to assess the adequacy of respirator fit that relies on the individual's response to the test agent.

Quantitative fit test (QNFT) means an assessment of the adequacy of respirator fit by numerically measuring the amount of leakage into the respirator.

Respiratory inlet covering means that portion of a respirator that forms the protective barrier between the user's respiratory tract and an air-purifying device or breathing air source, or both. It may be a facepiece, helmet, hood, suit, or a mouthpiece respirator with nose clamp.

Self-contained breathing apparatus (SCBA) means an atmosphere-supplying respirator for which the breathing air source is designed to be carried by the user.

Service life means the period of time that a respirator, filter or sorbent, or other respiratory equipment provides adequate protection to the wearer.

Supplied-air respirator (SAR) or airline respirator means an atmosphere-supplying respirator for which the source of breathing air is not designed to be carried by the user.

This section means this Respiratory Protection standard.

Tight-fitting facepiece means a respiratory inlet covering that forms a complete seal with the face.

User seal check means an action conducted by the respirator user to determine if the respirator is properly seated to the face.

1910.134(c)
Respiratory protection program.
This paragraph requires the employer to develop and implement a written respiratory protection program with required worksite-specific procedures and elements for required respirator use. The program must be administered by a suitably trained program administrator. In addition, certain program elements may be required for voluntary use to prevent potential hazards associated with the use of the respirator.

> Note: The *Small Entity Compliance Guide* contains criteria for the selection of a program administrator and a sample program that meets the requirements of this paragraph.

1910.134(c)(1)
In any workplace where respirators are necessary to protect the health of the employee or whenever respirators are required by the employer, the employer shall establish and implement a written respiratory protection program with worksite-specific procedures. The program shall be updated as necessary to reflect those changes in workplace conditions that affect respirator use. The employer shall include in the program the following provisions of this section, as applicable:

1910.134(c)(1)(i)
Procedures for selecting respirators for use in the workplace;

1910.134(c)(1)(ii)
Medical evaluations of employees required to use respirators;

1910.134(c)(1)(iii)
Fit testing procedures for tight-fitting respirators;

1910.134(c)(1)(iv)
Procedures for proper use of respirators in routine and reasonably foreseeable emergency situations;

1910.134(c)(1)(v)
Procedures and schedules for cleaning, disinfecting, storing, inspecting, repairing, discarding, and otherwise maintaining respirators;

1910.134(c)(1)(vi)
Procedures to ensure adequate air quality, quantity, and flow of breathing air for atmosphere-supplying respirators;

1910.134(c)(1)(vii)
Training of employees in the respiratory hazards to which they are potentially exposed during routine and emergency situations;

1910.134(c)(1)(viii)
Training of employees in the proper use of respirators, including putting on and removing them, any limitations on their use, and their maintenance; and

1910.134(c)(1)(ix)
Procedures for regularly evaluating the effectiveness of the program.

1910.134(c)(2)
Where respirator use is not required:

1910.134(c)(2)(i)
An employer may provide respirators at the request of employees or permit employees to use their own respirators, if the employer determines that such respirator use will not in itself create a hazard. If the employer determines that any voluntary respirator use is permissible, the employer shall provide the respirator users with the information contained in Appendix D to this section ("Information for Employees Using Respirators When Not Required Under the Standard"); and

1910.134(c)(2)(ii)
In addition, the employer must establish and implement those elements of a written respiratory protection program necessary to ensure that any employee using a respirator voluntarily is medically able to use that respirator, and that the respirator is cleaned, stored, and maintained so that its use does not present a health hazard to the user. Exception: Employers are not required to include in a written respiratory protection program those employees whose only use of respirators involves the voluntary use of filtering facepieces (dust masks).

1910.134(c)(3)
The employer shall designate a program administrator who is qualified by appropriate training or experience that is commensurate with the complexity of the program to administer or oversee the respiratory protection program and conduct the required evaluations of program effectiveness.

1910.134(c)(4)
The employer shall provide respirators, training, and medical evaluations at no cost to the employee.

1910.134(d)

Selection of respirators.

This paragraph requires the employer to evaluate respiratory hazard(s) in the workplace, identify relevant workplace and user factors, and base respirator selection on these factors. The paragraph also specifies appropriately protective respirators for use in IDLH atmospheres, and limits the selection and use of air-purifying respirators.

1910.134(d)(1

General requirements.

1910.134(d)(1)(i)

The employer shall select and provide an appropriate respirator based on the respiratory hazard(s) to which the worker is exposed and workplace and user factors that affect respirator performance and reliability.

1910.134(d)(1)(ii)

The employer shall select a NIOSH-certified respirator. The respirator shall be used in compliance with the conditions of its certification.

1910.134(d)(1)(iii)

The employer shall identify and evaluate the respiratory hazard(s) in the workplace; this evaluation shall include a reasonable estimate of employee exposures to respiratory hazard(s) and an identification of the contaminant's chemical state and physical form. Where the employer cannot identify or reasonably estimate the employee exposure, the employer shall consider the atmosphere to be IDLH.

1910.134(d)(1)(iv)

The employer shall select respirators from a sufficient number of respirator models and sizes so that the respirator is acceptable to, and correctly fits, the user.

1910.134(d)(2)

Respirators for IDLH atmospheres.

1910.134(d)(2)(i)

The employer shall provide the following respirators for employee use in IDLH atmospheres:

1910.134(d)(2)(i)(A)

A full facepiece pressure demand SCBA certified by NIOSH for a minimum service life of thirty minutes, or

1910.134(d)(2)(i)(B)

A combination full facepiece pressure demand supplied-air respirator (SAR) with auxiliary self-contained air supply.

1910.134(d)(2)(ii)

Respirators provided only for escape from IDLH atmospheres shall be NIOSH-certified for escape from the atmosphere in which they will be used.

1910.134(d)(2)(iii)

All oxygen-deficient atmospheres shall be considered IDLH. Exception: If the employer demonstrates that, under all foreseeable conditions, the oxygen concentration can be maintained within the ranges specified in Table II of this section (i.e., for the altitudes set out in the table), then any atmosphere-supplying respirator may be used.

1910.134(d)(3)

Respirators for atmospheres that are not IDLH.

1910.134(d)(3)(i)

The employer shall provide a respirator that is adequate to protect the health of the employee and ensure compliance with all other OSHA statutory and regulatory requirements, under routine and reasonably foreseeable emergency situations.

1910.134(d)(3)(i)(A)

Assigned Protection Factors (APFs) Employers must use the assigned protection factors listed in Table I to select a respirator that meets or exceeds the required level of employee protection. When using a combination respirator (e.g., airline respirators with an air-purifying filter), employers must ensure that the assigned protection factor is appropriate to the mode of operation in which the respirator is being used.

Table I: Assigned Protection Factors[5]

Type of Respirator[1,2]	Quarter mask	Half mask	Full facepiece	Helmet/Hood	Loose-fitting facepiece
1. Air-Purifying Respirator	5	10[3]	50	—	—
2. Powered Air-Purifying Respirator (PAPR)	—	50	1,000	25/1,000[4]	25
3. Supplied-Air Respirator (SAR) or Airline Respirator					
• Demand mode	—	10	50	—	—
• Continuous flow mode	—	50	1,000	25/1,000[4]	25
• Pressure-demand or other positive-pressure mode	—	50	1,000	—	—
4. Self-Contained Breathing Apparatus (SCBA)					
• Demand mode	—	10	50	50	—
• Pressure-demand or other positive-pressure mode (e.g., open/closed circuit)	—	—	10,000	10,000	—

Notes:

[1] Employers may select respirators assigned for use in higher workplace concentrations of a hazardous substance for use at lower concentrations of that substance, or when required respirator use is independent of concentration.

[2] The assigned protection factors in Table I are only effective when the employer implements a continuing, effective respirator program as required by this section (29 CFR 1910.134), including training, fit testing, maintenance, and use requirements.

[3] This APF category includes filtering facepieces, and half masks with elastomeric facepieces.

[4] The employer must have evidence provided by the respirator manufacturer that testing of these respirators demonstrates performance at a level of protection of 1,000 or greater to receive an APF of 1,000. This level of performance can best be demonstrated by performing a WPF or SWPF study or equivalent testing. Absent such testing, all other PAPRs and SARs with helmets/hoods are to be treated as loose-fitting facepiece respirators, and receive an APF of 25.

[5] These APFs do not apply to respirators used solely for escape. For escape respirators used in association with specific substances covered by 29 CFR 1910 subpart Z, employers must refer to the appropriate substance-specific standards in that subpart. Escape respirators for other IDLH atmospheres are specified by 29 CFR 1910.134(d)(2)(ii).

1910.134(d)(3)(i)(B)
Maximum Use Concentration (MUC)

1910.134(d)(3)(i)(B)(1)
The employer must select a respirator for employee use that maintains the employee's exposure to the hazardous substance, when measured outside the respirator, at or below the MUC.

1910.134(d)(3)(i)(B)(2)
Employers must not apply MUCs to conditions that are immediately dangerous to life or health (IDLH); instead, they must use respirators listed for IDLH conditions in paragraph (d)(2) of this standard.

1910.134(d)(3)(i)(B)(3)
When the calculated MUC exceeds the IDLH level for a hazardous substance, or the performance limits of the cartridge or canister, then employers must set the maximum MUC at that lower limit.

1910.134(d)(3)(ii)
The respirator selected shall be appropriate for the chemical state and physical form of the contaminant.

1910.134(d)(3)(iii)
For protection against gases and vapors, the employer shall provide:

1910.134(d)(3)(iii)(A)
An atmosphere-supplying respirator, or

1910.134(d)(3)(iii)(B)
An air-purifying respirator, provided that:

1910.134(d)(3)(iii)(B)(1)
The respirator is equipped with an end-of-service-life indicator (ESLI) certified by NIOSH for the contaminant; or

1910.134(d)(3)(iii)(B)(2)
If there is no ESLI appropriate for conditions in the employer's workplace, the employer implements a change schedule for canisters and cartridges that is based on objective information or data that will ensure that canisters and cartridges are changed before the end of their service life. The employer shall describe in the respirator program the information and data relied upon and the basis for the canister and

cartridge change schedule and the basis for reliance on the data.

1910.134(d)(3)(iv)
For protection against particulates, the employer shall provide:

1910.134(d)(3)(iv)(A)
An atmosphere-supplying respirator; or

1910.134(d)(3)(iv)(B)
An air-purifying respirator equipped with a filter certified by NIOSH under 30 CFR part 11 as a high efficiency particulate air (HEPA) filter, or an air-purifying respirator equipped with a filter certified for particulates by NIOSH under 42 CFR part 84; or

1910.134(d)(3)(iv)(C)
For contaminants consisting primarily of particles with mass median aerodynamic diameters (MMAD) of at least 2 micrometers, an air-purifying respirator equipped with any filter certified for particulates by NIOSH.

Table II: Oxygen Deficient Atmospheres	
Altitude (ft.)	Oxygen deficient atmospheres (% O_2) for which the employer may rely on atmosphere-supplying respirators
Less than 3,001	16.0-19.5
3,001-4,000	16.4-19.5
4,001-5,000	17.1-19.5
5,001-6,000	17.8-19.5
6,001-7,000	18.5-19.5
7,001-8,000[1]	19.3-19.5

[1] Above 8,000 feet the exception does not apply. Oxygen-enriched breathing air must be supplied above 14,000 feet.

1910.134(e)
Medical evaluation.
Using a respirator may place a physiological burden on employees that varies with the type of respirator worn, the job and workplace conditions in which the respirator is used, and the medical status of the employee. Accordingly, this paragraph specifies the minimum requirements for medical evaluation that employers must implement to determine the employee's ability to use a respirator.

1910.134(e)(1)
General. The employer shall provide a medical evaluation to determine the employee's ability to use a

respirator, before the employee is fit tested or required to use the respirator in the workplace. The employer may discontinue an employee's medical evaluations when the employee is no longer required to use a respirator.

1910.134(e)(2)
Medical evaluation procedures.

1910.134(e)(2)(i)
The employer shall identify a physician or other licensed health care professional (PLHCP) to perform medical evaluations using a medical questionnaire or an initial medical examination that obtains the same information as the medical questionnaire.

1910.134(e)(2)(ii)
The medical evaluation shall obtain the information requested by the questionnaire in Sections 1 and 2, Part A of Appendix C of this section.

1910.134(e)(3)
Follow-up medical examination.

1910.134(e)(3)(i)
The employer shall ensure that a follow-up medical examination is provided for an employee who gives a positive response to any question among questions 1 through 8 in Section 2, Part A of Appendix C or whose initial medical examination demonstrates the need for a follow-up medical examination.

1910.134(e)(3)(ii)
The follow-up medical examination shall include any medical tests, consultations, or diagnostic procedures that the PLHCP deems necessary to make a final determination.

1910.134(e)(4)
Administration of the medical questionnaire and examinations.

1910.134(e)(4)(i)
The medical questionnaire and examinations shall be administered confidentially during the employee's normal working hours or at a time and place convenient to the employee. The medical questionnaire shall be administered in a manner that ensures that the employee understands its content.

1910.134(e)(4)(ii)
The employer shall provide the employee with an opportunity to discuss the questionnaire and examination results with the PLHCP.

1910.134(e)(5)
Supplemental information for the PLHCP.

1910.134(e)(5)(i)
The following information must be provided to the PLHCP before the PLHCP makes a recommendation concerning an employee's ability to use a respirator:

1910.134(e)(5)(i)(A)
(A) The type and weight of the respirator to be used by the employee;

1910.134(e)(5)(i)(B)
The duration and frequency of respirator use (including use for rescue and escape);

1910.134(e)(5)(i)(C)
The expected physical work effort;

1910.134(e)(5)(i)(D)
Additional protective clothing and equipment to be worn; and

1910.134(e)(5)(i)(E)
Temperature and humidity extremes that may be encountered.

1910.134(e)(5)(ii)
Any supplemental information provided previously to the PLHCP regarding an employee need not be provided for a subsequent medical evaluation if the information and the PLHCP remain the same.

1910.134(e)(5)(iii)
The employer shall provide the PLHCP with a copy of the written respiratory protection program and a copy of this section.

Note to Paragraph (e)(5)(iii): When the employer replaces a PLHCP, the employer must ensure that the new PLHCP obtains this information, either by providing the documents directly to the PLHCP or having the documents transferred from the former PLHCP to the new PLHCP. However, OSHA does not expect employers to have employees medically reevaluated solely because a new PLHCP has been selected.

1910.134(e)(6)
Medical determination. In determining the employee's ability to use a respirator, the employer shall:

1910.134(e)(6)(i)
Obtain a written recommendation regarding the employee's ability to use the respirator from the PLHCP.

The recommendation shall provide only the following information:

1910.134(e)(6)(i)(A)
Any limitations on respirator use related to the medical condition of the employee, or relating to the workplace conditions in which the respirator will be used, including whether or not the employee is medically able to use the respirator;

1910.134(e)(6)(i)(B)
The need, if any, for follow-up medical evaluations; and

1910.134(e)(6)(i)(C)
A statement that the PLHCP has provided the employee with a copy of the PLHCP's written recommendation.

1910.134(e)(6)(ii)
If the respirator is a negative pressure respirator and the PLHCP finds a medical condition that may place the employee's health at increased risk if the respirator is used, the employer shall provide a PAPR if the PLHCP's medical evaluation finds that the employee can use such a respirator; if a subsequent medical evaluation finds that the employee is medically able to use a negative pressure respirator, then the employer is no longer required to provide a PAPR.

1910.134(e)(7)
Additional medical evaluations. At a minimum, the employer shall provide additional medical evaluations that comply with the requirements of this section if:

1910.134(e)(7)(i)
An employee reports medical signs or symptoms that are related to ability to use a respirator;

1910.134(e)(7)(ii)
A PLHCP, supervisor, or the respirator program administrator informs the employer that an employee needs to be reevaluated;

1910.134(e)(7)(iii)
Information from the respiratory protection program, including observations made during fit testing and program evaluation, indicates a need for employee reevaluation; or

1910.134(e)(7)(iv)
A change occurs in workplace conditions (e.g., physical work effort, protective clothing, temperature) that may result in a substantial increase in the physiological burden placed on an employee.

1910.134(f)
Fit testing.

This paragraph requires that, before an employee may be required to use any respirator with a negative or positive pressure tight-fitting facepiece, the employee must be fit tested with the same make, model, style, and size of respirator that will be used. This paragraph specifies the kinds of fit tests allowed, the procedures for conducting them, and how the results of the fit tests must be used.

1910.134(f)(1)

The employer shall ensure that employees using a tight-fitting facepiece respirator pass an appropriate qualitative fit test (QLFT) or quantitative fit test (QNFT) as stated in this paragraph.

1910.134(f)(2)

The employer shall ensure that an employee using a tight-fitting facepiece respirator is fit tested prior to initial use of the respirator, whenever a different respirator facepiece (size, style, model or make) is used, and at least annually thereafter.

1910.134(f)(3)

The employer shall conduct an additional fit test whenever the employee reports, or the employer, PLHCP, supervisor, or program administrator makes visual observations of, changes in the employee's physical condition that could affect respirator fit. Such conditions include, but are not limited to, facial scarring, dental changes, cosmetic surgery, or an obvious change in body weight.

1910.134(f)(4)

If after passing a QLFT or QNFT, the employee subsequently notifies the employer, program administrator, supervisor, or PLHCP that the fit of the respirator is unacceptable, the employee shall be given a reasonable opportunity to select a different respirator facepiece and to be retested.

1910.134(f)(5)

The fit test shall be administered using an OSHA-accepted QLFT or QNFT protocol. The OSHA-accepted QLFT and QNFT protocols and procedures are contained in Appendix A of this section.

1910.134(f)(6)

QLFT may only be used to fit test negative pressure air-purifying respirators that must achieve a fit factor of 100 or less.

1910.134(f)(7)

If the fit factor, as determined through an OSHA-accepted QNFT protocol, is equal to or greater than 100 for tight-fitting half facepieces, or equal to or greater

than 500 for tight-fitting full facepieces, the QNFT has been passed with that respirator.

1910.134(f)(8)

Fit testing of tight-fitting atmosphere-supplying respirators and tight-fitting powered air-purifying respirators shall be accomplished by performing quantitative or qualitative fit testing in the negative pressure mode, regardless of the mode of operation (negative or positive pressure) that is used for respiratory protection.

1910.134(f)(8)(i)

Qualitative fit testing of these respirators shall be accomplished by temporarily converting the respirator user's actual facepiece into a negative pressure respirator with appropriate filters, or by using an identical negative pressure air-purifying respirator facepiece with the same sealing surfaces as a surrogate for the atmosphere-supplying or powered air-purifying respirator facepiece.

1910.134(f)(8)(ii)

Quantitative fit testing of these respirators shall be accomplished by modifying the facepiece to allow sampling inside the facepiece in the breathing zone of the user, midway between the nose and mouth. This requirement shall be accomplished by installing a permanent sampling probe onto a surrogate facepiece, or by using a sampling adapter designed to temporarily provide a means of sampling air from inside the facepiece.

1910.134(f)(8)(iii)

Any modifications to the respirator facepiece for fit testing shall be completely removed, and the facepiece restored to NIOSH-approved configuration, before that facepiece can be used in the workplace.

1910.134(g)
Use of respirators.

This paragraph requires employers to establish and implement procedures for the proper use of respirators. These requirements include prohibiting conditions that may result in facepiece seal leakage, preventing employees from removing respirators in hazardous environments, taking actions to ensure continued effective respirator operation throughout the work shift, and establishing procedures for the use of respirators in IDLH atmospheres or in interior structural firefighting situations.

1910.134(g)(1)
Facepiece seal protection.
1910.134(g)(1)(i)

The employer shall not permit respirators with tight-fitting facepieces to be worn by employees who have:

1910.134(g)(1)(i)(A)
Facial hair that comes between the sealing surface of the facepiece and the face or that interferes with valve function; or

1910.134(g)(1)(i)(B)
Any condition that interferes with the face-to-facepiece seal or valve function.

1910.134(g)(1)(ii)
If an employee wears corrective glasses or goggles or other personal protective equipment, the employer shall ensure that such equipment is worn in a manner that does not interfere with the seal of the facepiece to the face of the user.

1910.134(g)(1)(iii)
For all tight-fitting respirators, the employer shall ensure that employees perform a user seal check each time they put on the respirator using the procedures in Appendix B-1 or procedures recommended by the respirator manufacturer that the employer demonstrates are as effective as those in Appendix B-1 of this section.

1910.134(g)(2)
Continuing respirator effectiveness.
1910.134(g)(2)(i)
Appropriate surveillance shall be maintained of work area conditions and degree of employee exposure or stress. When there is a change in work area conditions or degree of employee exposure or stress that may affect respirator effectiveness, the employer shall reevaluate the continued effectiveness of the respirator.

1910.134(g)(2)(ii)
The employer shall ensure that employees leave the respirator use area:

1910.134(g)(2)(ii)(A)
To wash their faces and respirator facepieces as necessary to prevent eye or skin irritation associated with respirator use; or

1910.134(g)(2)(ii)(B)
If they detect vapor or gas breakthrough, changes in breathing resistance, or leakage of the facepiece; or

1910.134(g)(2)(ii)(C)
To replace the respirator or the filter, cartridge, or canister elements.

1910.134(g)(2)(iii)
If the employee detects vapor or gas breakthrough, changes in breathing resistance, or leakage of the facepiece, the employer must replace or repair the

respirator before allowing the employee to return to the work area.

1910.134(g)(3)
Procedures for IDLH atmospheres. For all IDLH atmospheres, the employer shall ensure that:

1910.134(g)(3)(i)
One employee or, when needed, more than one employee is located outside the IDLH atmosphere;

1910.134(g)(3)(ii)
Visual, voice, or signal line communication is maintained between the employee(s) in the IDLH atmosphere and the employee(s) located outside the IDLH atmosphere;

1910.134(g)(3)(iii)
The employee(s) located outside the IDLH atmosphere are trained and equipped to provide effective emergency rescue;

1910.134(g)(3)(iv)
The employer or designee is notified before the employee(s) located outside the IDLH atmosphere enter the IDLH atmosphere to provide emergency rescue;

1910.134(g)(3)(v)
The employer or designee authorized to do so by the employer, once notified, provides necessary assistance appropriate to the situation;

1910.134(g)(3)(vi)
Employee(s) located outside the IDLH atmospheres are equipped with:

1910.134(g)(3)(vi)(A)
Pressure demand or other positive pressure SCBAs, or a pressure demand or other positive pressure supplied-air respirator with auxiliary SCBA; and either

1910.134(g)(3)(vi)(B)
Appropriate retrieval equipment for removing the employee(s) who enter(s) these hazardous atmospheres where retrieval equipment would contribute to the rescue of the employee(s) and would not increase the overall risk resulting from entry; or

1910.134(g)(3)(vi)(C)
Equivalent means for rescue where retrieval equipment is not required under paragraph (g)(3)(vi)(B).

1910.134(g)(4)
Procedures for interior structural firefighting. In addition to the requirements set forth under paragraph (g)(3), in interior structural fires, the employer shall ensure that:

1910.134(g)(4)(i)
At least two employees enter the IDLH atmosphere and remain in visual or voice contact with one another at all times;

1910.134(g)(4)(ii)
At least two employees are located outside the IDLH atmosphere; and

1910.134(g)(4)(iii)
All employees engaged in interior structural firefighting use SCBAs.

Note 1 to paragraph (g): One of the two individuals located outside the IDLH atmosphere may be assigned to an additional role, such as incident commander in charge of the emergency or safety officer, so long as this individual is able to perform assistance or rescue activities without jeopardizing the safety or health of any firefighter working at the incident.

Note 2 to paragraph (g): Nothing in this section is meant to preclude firefighters from performing emergency rescue activities before an entire team has assembled.

1910.134(h)
Maintenance and care of respirators.
This paragraph requires the employer to provide for the cleaning and disinfecting, storage, inspection, and repair of respirators used by employees.

1910.134(h)(1)
Cleaning and disinfecting. The employer shall provide each respirator user with a respirator that is clean, sanitary, and in good working order. The employer shall ensure that respirators are cleaned and disinfected using the procedures in Appendix B-2 of this section, or procedures recommended by the respirator manufacturer, provided that such procedures are of equivalent effectiveness. The respirators shall be cleaned and disinfected at the following intervals:

1910.134(h)(1)(i)
Respirators issued for the exclusive use of an employee shall be cleaned and disinfected as often as necessary to be maintained in a sanitary condition;

1910.134(h)(1)(ii)
Respirators issued to more than one employee shall be cleaned and disinfected before being worn by different individuals;

1910.134(h)(1)(iii)
Respirators maintained for emergency use shall be cleaned and disinfected after each use; and

1910.134(h)(1)(iv)
Respirators used in fit testing and training shall be cleaned and disinfected after each use.

1910.134(h)(2)
Storage. The employer shall ensure that respirators are stored as follows:

1910.134(h)(2)(i)
All respirators shall be stored to protect them from damage, contamination, dust, sunlight, extreme temperatures, excessive moisture, and damaging chemicals, and they shall be packed or stored to prevent deformation of the facepiece and exhalation valve.

1910.134(h)(2)(ii)
In addition to the requirements of paragraph (h)(2)(i) of this section, emergency respirators shall be:

1910.134(h)(2)(ii)(A)
Kept accessible to the work area;

1910.134(h)(2)(ii)(B)
Stored in compartments or in covers that are clearly marked as containing emergency respirators; and

1910.134(h)(2)(ii)(C)
Stored in accordance with any applicable manufacturer instructions.

1910.134(h)(3)
Inspection.

1910.134(h)(3)(i)
The employer shall ensure that respirators are inspected as follows:

1910.134(h)(3)(i)(A)
All respirators used in routine situations shall be inspected before each use and during cleaning;

1910.134(h)(3)(i)(B)
All respirators maintained for use in emergency situations shall be inspected at least monthly and in accordance with the manufacturer's recommendations, and shall be checked for proper function before and after each use; and

1910.134(h)(3)(i)(C)
Emergency escape-only respirators shall be inspected before being carried into the workplace for use.

1910.134(h)(3)(ii)
The employer shall ensure that respirator inspections include the following:

1910.134(h)(3)(ii)(A)

A check of respirator function, tightness of connections, and the condition of the various parts including, but not limited to, the facepiece, head straps, valves, connecting tube, and cartridges, canisters or filters; and

1910.134(h)(3)(ii)(B)

A check of elastomeric parts for pliability and signs of deterioration.

1910.134(h)(3)(iii)

In addition to the requirements of paragraphs (h)(3)(i) and (ii) of this section, self-contained breathing apparatus shall be inspected monthly. Air and oxygen cylinders shall be maintained in a fully charged state and shall be recharged when the pressure falls to 90% of the manufacturer's recommended pressure level. The employer shall determine that the regulator and warning devices function properly.

1910.134(h)(3)(iv)

For respirators maintained for emergency use, the employer shall:

1910.134(h)(3)(iv)(A)

Certify the respirator by documenting the date the inspection was performed, the name (or signature) of the person who made the inspection, the findings, required remedial action, and a serial number or other means of identifying the inspected respirator; and

1910.134(h)(3)(iv)(B)

Provide this information on a tag or label that is attached to the storage compartment for the respirator, is kept with the respirator, or is included in inspection reports stored as paper or electronic files. This information shall be maintained until replaced following a subsequent certification.

1910.134(h)(4)

Repairs. The employer shall ensure that respirators that fail an inspection or are otherwise found to be defective are removed from service, and are discarded or repaired or adjusted in accordance with the following procedures:

1910.134(h)(4)(i)

Repairs or adjustments to respirators are to be made only by persons appropriately trained to perform such operations and shall use only the respirator manufacturer's NIOSH-approved parts designed for the respirator;

1910.134(h)(4)(ii)

Repairs shall be made according to the manufacturer's recommendations and specifications for the type and extent of repairs to be performed; and

1910.134(h)(4)(iii)

Reducing and admission valves, regulators, and alarms shall be adjusted or repaired only by the manufacturer or a technician trained by the manufacturer.

1910.134(i)
Breathing air quality and use.
This paragraph requires the employer to provide employees using atmosphere-supplying respirators (supplied-air and SCBA) with breathing gases of high purity.

1910.134(i)(1)

The employer shall ensure that compressed air, compressed oxygen, liquid air, and liquid oxygen used for respiration accords with the following specifications:

1910.134(i)(1)(i)

Compressed and liquid oxygen shall meet the United States Pharmacopoeia requirements for medical or breathing oxygen; and

1910.134(i)(1)(ii)

Compressed breathing air shall meet at least the requirements for Grade D breathing air described in ANSI/Compressed Gas Association Commodity Specification for Air, G-7.1-1989, to include:

1910.134(i)(1)(ii)(A)

Oxygen content (v/v) of 19.5-23.5%;

1910.134(i)(1)(ii)(B)

Hydrocarbon (condensed) content of 5 milligrams per cubic meter of air or less;

1910.134(i)(1)(ii)(C)

Carbon monoxide (CO) content of 10 ppm or less;

1910.134(i)(1)(ii)(D)

Carbon dioxide content of 1,000 ppm or less; and

1910.134(i)(1)(ii)(E)

Lack of noticeable odor.

1910.134(i)(2)

The employer shall ensure that compressed oxygen is not used in atmosphere-supplying respirators that have previously used compressed air.

1910.134(i)(3)
The employer shall ensure that oxygen concentrations greater than 23.5% are used only in equipment designed for oxygen service or distribution.

1910.134(i)(4)
The employer shall ensure that cylinders used to supply breathing air to respirators meet the following requirements:

1910.134(i)(4)(i)
Cylinders are tested and maintained as prescribed in the Shipping Container Specification Regulations of the Department of Transportation (49 CFR part 173 and part 178);

1910.134(i)(4)(ii)
Cylinders of purchased breathing air have a certificate of analysis from the supplier that the breathing air meets the requirements for Grade D breathing air; and

1910.134(i)(4)(iii)
The moisture content in the cylinder does not exceed a dew point of -50 deg.F (-45.6 deg.C) at 1 atmosphere pressure.

1910.134(i)(5)
The employer shall ensure that compressors used to supply breathing air to respirators are constructed and situated so as to:

1910.134(i)(5)(i)
Prevent entry of contaminated air into the air-supply system;

1910.134(i)(5)(ii)
Minimize moisture content so that the dew point at 1 atmosphere pressure is 10 degrees F (5.56 deg.C) below the ambient temperature;

1910.134(i)(5)(iii)
Have suitable in-line air-purifying sorbent beds and filters to further ensure breathing air quality. Sorbent beds and filters shall be maintained and replaced or refurbished periodically following the manufacturer's instructions.

1910.134(i)(5)(iv)
Have a tag containing the most recent change date and the signature of the person authorized by the employer to perform the change. The tag shall be maintained at the compressor.

1910.134(i)(6)
For compressors that are not oil-lubricated, the employer shall ensure that carbon monoxide levels in the breathing air do not exceed 10 ppm.

1910.134(i)(7)
For oil-lubricated compressors, the employer shall use a high-temperature or carbon monoxide alarm, or both, to monitor carbon monoxide levels. If only high-temperature alarms are used, the air supply shall be monitored at intervals sufficient to prevent carbon monoxide in the breathing air from exceeding 10 ppm.

1910.134(i)(8)
The employer shall ensure that breathing air couplings are incompatible with outlets for nonrespirable worksite air or other gas systems. No asphyxiating substance shall be introduced into breathing air lines.

1910.134(i)(9)
The employer shall use breathing gas containers marked in accordance with the NIOSH respirator certification standard, 42 CFR part 84.

1910.134(j)
Identification of filters, cartridges, and canisters.
The employer shall ensure that all filters, cartridges and canisters used in the workplace are labeled and color coded with the NIOSH approval label and that the label is not removed and remains legible.

1910.134(k)
Training and information.
This paragraph requires the employer to provide effective training to employees who are required to use respirators. The training must be comprehensive, understandable, and recur annually, and more often if necessary. This paragraph also requires the employer to provide the basic information on respirators in Appendix D of this section to employees who wear respirators when not required by this section or by the employer to do so.

1910.134(k)(1)
The employer shall ensure that each employee can demonstrate knowledge of at least the following:

1910.134(k)(1)(i)
Why the respirator is necessary and how improper fit, usage, or maintenance can compromise the protective effect of the respirator;

1910.134(k)(1)(ii)
What the limitations and capabilities of the respirator are;

1910.134(k)(1)(iii)
How to use the respirator effectively in emergency situations, including situations in which the respirator malfunctions;

1910.134(k)(1)(iv)
How to inspect, put on and remove, use, and check the seals of the respirator;

1910.134(k)(1)(v)
What the procedures are for maintenance and storage of the respirator;

1910.134(k)(1)(vi)
How to recognize medical signs and symptoms that may limit or prevent the effective use of respirators; and

1910.134(k)(1)(vii)
The general requirements of this section.

1910.134(k)(2)
The training shall be conducted in a manner that is understandable to the employee.

1910.134(k)(3)
The employer shall provide the training prior to requiring the employee to use a respirator in the workplace.

1910.134(k)(4)
An employer who is able to demonstrate that a new employee has received training within the last 12 months that addresses the elements specified in paragraph (k)(1)(i) through (vii) is not required to repeat such training provided that, as required by paragraph (k)(1), the employee can demonstrate knowledge of those element(s). Previous training not repeated initially by the employer must be provided no later than 12 months from the date of the previous training.

1910.134(k)(5)
Retraining shall be administered annually, and when the following situations occur:

1910.134(k)(5)(i)
Changes in the workplace or the type of respirator render previous training obsolete;

1910.134(k)(5)(ii)
Inadequacies in the employee's knowledge or use of the respirator indicate that the employee has not retained the requisite understanding or skill; or

1910.134(k)(5)(iii)
Any other situation arises in which retraining appears necessary to ensure safe respirator use.

1910.134(k)(6)
The basic advisory information on respirators, as presented in Appendix D of this section, shall be provided by the employer in any written or oral format, to employees who wear respirators when such use is not required by this section or by the employer.

1910.134(l)
Program evaluation.
This section requires the employer to conduct evaluations of the workplace to ensure that the written respiratory protection program is being properly implemented, and to consult employees to ensure that they are using the respirators properly.

1910.134(l)(1)
The employer shall conduct evaluations of the workplace as necessary to ensure that the provisions of the current written program are being effectively implemented and that it continues to be effective.

1910.134(l)(2)
The employer shall regularly consult employees required to use respirators to assess the employees' views on program effectiveness and to identify any problems. Any problems that are identified during this assessment shall be corrected. Factors to be assessed include, but are not limited to:

1910.134(l)(2)(i)
Respirator fit (including the ability to use the respirator without interfering with effective workplace performance);

1910.134(l)(2)(ii)
Appropriate respirator selection for the hazards to which the employee is exposed;

1910.134(l)(2)(iii)
Proper respirator use under the workplace conditions the employee encounters; and

1910.134(l)(2)(iv)
Proper respirator maintenance.

1910.134(m)
Recordkeeping.
This section requires the employer to establish and retain written information regarding medical evaluations, fit testing, and the respirator program. This in-

formation will facilitate employee involvement in the respirator program, assist the employer in auditing the adequacy of the program, and provide a record for compliance determinations by OSHA.

1910.134(m)(1)
Medical evaluation. Records of medical evaluations required by this section must be retained and made available in accordance with 29 CFR 1910.1020.

1910.134(m)(2)
Fit testing.

1910.134(m)(2)(i)
The employer shall establish a record of the qualitative and quantitative fit tests administered to an employee including:

1910.134(m)(2)(i)(A)
The name or identification of the employee tested;

1910.134(m)(2)(i)(B)
Type of fit test performed;

1910.134(m)(2)(i)(C)
Specific make, model, style, and size of respirator tested;

1910.134(m)(2)(i)(D)
Date of test; and

1910.134(m)(2)(i)(E)
The pass/fail results for QLFTs or the fit factor and strip chart recording or other recording of the test results for QNFTs.

1910.134(m)(2)(ii)
Fit test records shall be retained for respirator users until the next fit test is administered.

1910.134(m)(3)
A written copy of the current respirator program shall be retained by the employer.

1910.134(m)(4)
Written materials required to be retained under this paragraph shall be made available upon request to affected employees and to the Assistant Secretary or designee for examination and copying.

1910.134(n)
Effective date.
Paragraphs (d)(3)(i)(A) and (d)(3)(i)(B) of this section become effective November 22, 2006.

1910.134(o)
Appendices.

1910.134(o)(1)
Compliance with Appendix A, Appendix B-1, Appendix B-2, and Appendix C of this section is mandatory.

1910.134(o)(2)
Appendix D of this section is non-mandatory and is not intended to create any additional obligations not otherwise imposed or to detract from any existing obligations.

[63 FR 1152, Jan. 8, 1998; 63 FR 20098, April 23, 1998; 71 FR 16672, April 3, 2006; 71 FR 50187, August 24, 2006]

Appendix A to §1910.134: Fit Testing Procedures (Mandatory)

Part I. OSHA-Accepted Fit Test Protocols

A. Fit Testing Procedures -- General Requirements

The employer shall conduct fit testing using the following procedures. The requirements in this appendix apply to all OSHA-accepted fit test methods, both QLFT and QNFT.

1. The test subject shall be allowed to pick the most acceptable respirator from a sufficient number of respirator models and sizes so that the respirator is acceptable to, and correctly fits, the user.

2. Prior to the selection process, the test subject shall be shown how to put on a respirator, how it should be positioned on the face, how to set strap tension and how to determine an acceptable fit. A mirror shall be available to assist the subject in evaluating the fit and positioning of the respirator. This instruction may not constitute the subject's formal training on respirator use, because it is only a review.

3. The test subject shall be informed that he/she is being asked to select the respirator that provides the most acceptable fit. Each respirator represents a different size and shape, and if fitted and used properly, will provide adequate protection.

4. The test subject shall be instructed to hold each chosen facepiece up to the face and eliminate those that obviously do not give an acceptable fit.

5. The more acceptable facepieces are noted in case the one selected proves unacceptable; the most comfortable mask is donned and worn at least five minutes to assess comfort. Assistance in assessing comfort can be given by discussing the points in the following item A.6. If the test subject is not familiar with using a particular respirator, the test subject shall be directed to don the mask several times and to adjust the straps each time to become adept at setting proper tension on the straps.

6. Assessment of comfort shall include a review of the following points with the test subject and allowing the test subject adequate time to determine the comfort of the respirator:
   (a) Position of the mask on the nose
   (b) Room for eye protection
   (c) Room to talk
   (d) Position of mask on face and cheeks

7. The following criteria shall be used to help determine the adequacy of the respirator fit:
   (a) Chin properly placed;
   (b) Adequate strap tension, not overly tightened;
   (c) Fit across nose bridge;
   (d) Respirator of proper size to span distance from nose to chin;
   (e) Tendency of respirator to slip;
   (f) Self-observation in mirror to evaluate fit and respirator position.

8. The test subject shall conduct a user seal check, either the negative and positive pressure seal checks described in Appendix B-1 of this section or those recommended by the respirator manufacturer which provide equivalent protection to the procedures in Appendix B-1. Before conducting the negative and positive pressure checks, the subject shall be told to seat the mask on the face by moving the head from side-to-side and up and down slowly while taking in a few slow deep breaths. Another facepiece shall be selected and retested if the test subject fails the user seal check tests.

9. The test shall not be conducted if there is any hair growth between the skin and the facepiece sealing surface, such as stubble beard growth, beard, mustache or sideburns which cross the respirator sealing surface. Any type of apparel which interferes with a satisfactory fit shall be altered or removed.

10. If a test subject exhibits difficulty in breathing during the tests, she or he shall be referred to a physician or other licensed health care professional, as appropriate, to determine whether the test subject can wear a respirator while performing her or his duties.

11. If the employee finds the fit of the respirator unacceptable, the test subject shall be given the opportunity to select a different respirator and to be retested.

12. Exercise regimen. Prior to the commencement of the fit test, the test subject shall be given a description of the fit test and the test subject's responsibilities during the test procedure. The description of the process shall include a description of the test exercises that the subject will be performing. The respirator to be tested shall be worn for at least 5 minutes before the start of the fit test.

13. The fit test shall be performed while the test subject is wearing any applicable safety equipment that may be worn during actual respirator use which could interfere with respirator fit.

OSHA®
www.osha.gov
Occupational Safety and Health Administration

14. Test Exercises.

(a) Employers must perform the following test exercises for all fit testing methods prescribed in this appendix, except for the CNP quantitative fit testing protocol and the CNP REDON quantitative fit testing protocol. For these two protocols, employers must ensure that the test subjects (i.e., employees) perform the exercise procedure specified in Part I.C.4(b) of this appendix for the CNP quantitative fit testing protocol, or the exercise procedure described in Part I.C.5(b) of this appendix for the CNP REDON quantitative fit-testing protocol. For the remaining fit testing methods, employers must ensure that employees perform the test exercises in the appropriate test environment in the following manner:

(1) Normal breathing. In a normal standing position, without talking, the subject shall breathe normally.

(2) Deep breathing. In a normal standing position, the subject shall breathe slowly and deeply, taking caution so as not to hyperventilate.

(3) Turning head side to side. Standing in place, the subject shall slowly turn his/her head from side to side between the extreme positions on each side. The head shall be held at each extreme momentarily so the subject can inhale at each side.

(4) Moving head up and down. Standing in place, the subject shall slowly move his/her head up and down. The subject shall be instructed to inhale in the up position (i.e., when looking toward the ceiling).

(5) Talking. The subject shall talk out loud slowly and loud enough so as to be heard clearly by the test conductor. The subject can read from a prepared text such as the Rainbow Passage, count backward from 100, or recite a memorized poem or song.

Rainbow Passage

When the sunlight strikes raindrops in the air, they act like a prism and form a rainbow. The rainbow is a division of white light into many beautiful colors. These take the shape of a long round arch, with its path high above, and its two ends apparently beyond the horizon. There is, according to legend, a boiling pot of gold at one end. People look, but no one ever finds it. When a man looks for something beyond reach, his friends say he is looking for the pot of gold at the end of the rainbow.

(6) Grimace. The test subject shall grimace by smiling or frowning. (This applies only to QNFT testing; it is not performed for QLFT)

(7) Bending over. The test subject shall bend at the waist as if he/she were to touch his/her toes. Jogging in place shall be substituted for this exercise in those test environments such as shroud type QNFT or QLFT units that do not permit bending over at the waist.

(8) Normal breathing. Same as exercise (1).

(b) Each test exercise shall be performed for one minute except for the grimace exercise which shall be performed for 15 seconds. The test subject shall be questioned by the test conductor regarding the comfort of the respirator upon completion of the protocol. If it has become unacceptable, another model of respirator shall be tried. The respirator shall not be adjusted once the fit test exercises begin. Any adjustment voids the test, and the fit test must be repeated.

B. Qualitative Fit Test (QLFT) Protocols

1. General

(a) The employer shall ensure that persons administering QLFT are able to prepare test solutions, calibrate equipment and perform tests properly, recognize invalid tests, and ensure that test equipment is in proper working order.

(b) The employer shall ensure that QLFT equipment is kept clean and well maintained so as to operate within the parameters for which it was designed.

2. Isoamyl Acetate Protocol

Note: This protocol is not appropriate to use for the fit testing of particulate respirators. If used to fit test particulate respirators, the respirator must be equipped with an organic vapor filter.

(a) Odor Threshold Screening

Odor threshold screening, performed without wearing a respirator, is intended to determine if the individual tested can detect the odor of isoamyl acetate at low levels.

(1) Three 1 liter glass jars with metal lids are required.

(2) Odor-free water (e.g., distilled or spring water) at approximately 25 deg. C (77 deg. F) shall be used for the solutions.

(3) The isoamyl acetate (IAA) (also known at isopentyl acetate) stock solution is prepared by adding 1 ml of pure IAA to 800 ml of odor-free water in a 1 liter jar, closing the lid and shaking for 30 seconds. A new solution shall be prepared at least weekly.

(4) The screening test shall be conducted in a room separate from the room used for actual fit testing. The two rooms shall be well-ventilated to prevent the odor of IAA from becoming evident in the general room air where testing takes place.

(5) The odor test solution is prepared in a second jar by placing 0.4 ml of the stock solution into 500 ml of odor-free water using a clean dropper or pipette. The solution shall be shaken for 30 seconds and allowed to stand for two to three minutes so that the IAA concentration above the liquid may reach equilibrium. This solution shall be used for only one day.

(6) A test blank shall be prepared in a third jar by adding 500 cc of odor-free water.

(7) The odor test and test blank jar lids shall be labeled (e.g., 1 and 2) for jar identification. Labels shall be placed on the lids so that they can be peeled off periodically and switched to maintain the integrity of the test.

(8) The following instruction shall be typed on a card and placed on the table in front of the two test jars (i.e., 1 and 2): "The purpose of this test is to determine if you can smell banana oil at a low concentration. The two bottles in front of you contain water. One of these bottles also contains a small amount of banana oil. Be sure the covers are on tight, then shake each bottle for two seconds. Unscrew the lid of each bottle, one at a time, and sniff at the mouth of the bottle. Indicate to the test conductor which bottle contains banana oil."

(9) The mixtures used in the IAA odor detection test shall be prepared in an area separate from where the test is performed, in order to prevent olfactory fatigue in the subject.

(10) If the test subject is unable to correctly identify the jar containing the odor test solution, the IAA qualitative fit test shall not be performed.

(11) If the test subject correctly identifies the jar containing the odor test solution, the test subject may proceed to respirator selection and fit testing.

(b) Isoamyl Acetate Fit Test

(1) The fit test chamber shall be a clear 55-gallon drum liner suspended inverted over a 2-foot diameter frame so that the top of the chamber is about 6 inches above the test subject's head. If no drum liner is available, a similar chamber shall be constructed using plastic sheeting. The inside top center of the chamber shall have a small hook attached.

(2) Each respirator used for the fitting and fit testing shall be equipped with organic vapor cartridges or offer protection against organic vapors.

(3) After selecting, donning, and properly adjusting a respirator, the test subject shall wear it to the fit testing room. This room shall be separate from the room used for odor threshold screening and respirator selection, and shall be well-ventilated, as by an exhaust fan or lab hood, to prevent general room contamination.

(4) A copy of the test exercises and any prepared text from which the subject is to read shall be taped to the inside of the test chamber.

(5) Upon entering the test chamber, the test subject shall be given a 6-inch by 5-inch piece of paper towel, or other porous, absorbent, singleply material, folded in half and wetted with 0.75 ml of pure IAA. The test subject shall hang the wet towel on the hook at the top of the chamber. An IAA test swab or ampule may be substituted for the IAA wetted paper towel provided it has been demonstrated that the alternative IAA source will generate an IAA test atmosphere with a concentration equivalent to that generated by the paper towel method.

(6) Allow two minutes for the IAA test concentration to stabilize before starting the fit test exercises. This would be an appropriate time to talk with the test subject; to explain the fit test, the importance of his/her cooperation, and the purpose for the test exercises; or to demonstrate some of the exercises.

(7) If at any time during the test, the subject detects the banana-like odor of IAA, the test is failed. The subject shall quickly exit from the

test chamber and leave the test area to avoid olfactory fatigue.

(8) If the test is failed, the subject shall return to the selection room and remove the respirator. The test subject shall repeat the odor sensitivity test, select and put on another respirator, return to the test area and again begin the fit test procedure described in (b) (1) through (7) above. The process continues until a respirator that fits well has been found. Should the odor sensitivity test be failed, the subject shall wait at least 5 minutes before retesting. Odor sensitivity will usually have returned by this time.

(9) If the subject passes the test, the efficiency of the test procedure shall be demonstrated by having the subject break the respirator face seal and take a breath before exiting the chamber.

(10) When the test subject leaves the chamber, the subject shall remove the saturated towel and return it to the person conducting the test, so that there is no significant IAA concentration buildup in the chamber during subsequent tests. The used towels shall be kept in a self-sealing plastic bag to keep the test area from being contaminated.

3. Saccharin Solution Aerosol Protocol

The entire screening and testing procedure shall be explained to the test subject prior to the conduct of the screening test.

(a) Taste threshold screening. The saccharin taste threshold screening, performed without wearing a respirator, is intended to determine whether the individual being tested can detect the taste of saccharin.

(1) During threshold screening as well as during fit testing, subjects shall wear an enclosure about the head and shoulders that is approximately 12 inches in diameter by 14 inches tall with at least the front portion clear and that allows free movements of the head when a respirator is worn. An enclosure substantially similar to the 3M hood assembly, parts # FT 14 and # FT 15 combined, is adequate.

(2) The test enclosure shall have a 3/4-inch (1.9 cm) hole in front of the test subject's nose and mouth area to accommodate the nebulizer nozzle.

(3) The test subject shall don the test enclosure.

Throughout the threshold screening test, the test subject shall breathe through his/her slightly open mouth with tongue extended. The subject is instructed to report when he/she detects a sweet taste.

(4) Using a DeVilbiss Model 40 Inhalation Medication Nebulizer or equivalent, the test conductor shall spray the threshold check solution into the enclosure. The nozzle is directed away from the nose and mouth of the person. This nebulizer shall be clearly marked to distinguish it from the fit test solution nebulizer.

(5) The threshold check solution is prepared by dissolving 0.83 gram of sodium saccharin USP in 100 ml of warm water. It can be prepared by putting 1 ml of the fit test solution (see (b)(5) below) in 100 ml of distilled water.

(6) To produce the aerosol, the nebulizer bulb is firmly squeezed so that it collapses completely, then released and allowed to fully expand.

(7) Ten squeezes are repeated rapidly and then the test subject is asked whether the saccharin can be tasted. If the test subject reports tasting the sweet taste during the ten squeezes, the screening test is completed. The taste threshold is noted as ten regardless of the number of squeezes actually completed.

(8) If the first response is negative, ten more squeezes are repeated rapidly and the test subject is again asked whether the saccharin is tasted. If the test subject reports tasting the sweet taste during the second ten squeezes, the screening test is completed. The taste threshold is noted as twenty regardless of the number of squeezes actually completed.

(9) If the second response is negative, ten more squeezes are repeated rapidly and the test subject is again asked whether the saccharin is tasted. If the test subject reports tasting the sweet taste during the third set of ten squeezes, the screening test is completed. The taste threshold is noted as thirty regardless of the number of squeezes actually completed.

(10) The test conductor will take note of the number of squeezes required to solicit a taste response.

(11) If the saccharin is not tasted after 30 squeezes (step 10), the test subject is unable to taste saccharin and may not perform the sac-

charin fit test.

Note to paragraph 3. (a): If the test subject eats or drinks something sweet before the screening test, he/she may be unable to taste the weak saccharin solution.

(12) If a taste response is elicited, the test subject shall be asked to take note of the taste for reference in the fit test.

(13) Correct use of the nebulizer means that approximately 1 ml of liquid is used at a time in the nebulizer body.

(14) The nebulizer shall be thoroughly rinsed in water, shaken dry, and refilled at least each morning and afternoon or at least every four hours.

(b) Saccharin solution aerosol fit test procedure.

(1) The test subject may not eat, drink (except plain water), smoke, or chew gum for 15 minutes before the test.

(2) The fit test uses the same enclosure described in 3. (a) above.

(3) The test subject shall don the enclosure while wearing the respirator selected in section I. A. of this appendix. The respirator shall be properly adjusted and equipped with a particulate filter(s).

(4) A second DeVilbiss Model 40 Inhalation Medication Nebulizer or equivalent is used to spray the fit test solution into the enclosure. This nebulizer shall be clearly marked to distinguish it from the screening test solution nebulizer.

(5) The fit test solution is prepared by adding 83 grams of sodium saccharin to 100 ml of warm water.

(6) As before, the test subject shall breathe through the slightly open mouth with tongue extended, and report if he/she tastes the sweet taste of saccharin.

(7) The nebulizer is inserted into the hole in the front of the enclosure and an initial concentration of saccharin fit test solution is sprayed into the enclosure using the same number of squeezes (either 10, 20 or 30 squeezes) based on the number of squeezes required to elicit a taste

response as noted during the screening test. A minimum of 10 squeezes is required.

(8) After generating the aerosol, the test subject shall be instructed to perform the exercises in section I. A. 14. of this appendix.

(9) Every 30 seconds the aerosol concentration shall be replenished using one half the original number of squeezes used initially (e.g., 5, 10 or 15).

(10) The test subject shall indicate to the test conductor if at any time during the fit test the taste of saccharin is detected. If the test subject does not report tasting the saccharin, the test is passed.

(11) If the taste of saccharin is detected, the fit is deemed unsatisfactory and the test is failed. A different respirator shall be tried and the entire test procedure is repeated (taste threshold screening and fit testing).

(12) Since the nebulizer has a tendency to clog during use, the test operator must make periodic checks of the nebulizer to ensure that it is not clogged. If clogging is found at the end of the test session, the test is invalid.

4. BitrexTM (Denatonium Benzoate) Solution Aerosol Qualitative Fit Test Protocol

The BitrexTM (Denatonium benzoate) solution aerosol QLFT protocol uses the published saccharin test protocol because that protocol is widely accepted. Bitrex is routinely used as a taste aversion agent in household liquids which children should not be drinking and is endorsed by the American Medical Association, the National Safety Council, and the American Association of Poison Control Centers. The entire screening and testing procedure shall be explained to the test subject prior to the conduct of the screening test.

(a) Taste Threshold Screening.

The Bitrex taste threshold screening, performed without wearing a respirator, is intended to determine whether the individual being tested can detect the taste of Bitrex.

(1) During threshold screening as well as during fit testing, subjects shall wear an enclosure about the head and shoulders that is approximately 12 inches (30.5 cm) in diameter by 14 inches (35.6 cm) tall. The front portion of the en-

closure shall be clear from the respirator and allow free movement of the head when a respirator is worn. An enclosure substantially similar to the 3M hood assembly, parts # FT 14 and # FT 15 combined, is adequate.

(2) The test enclosure shall have a 3/4 inch (1.9 cm) hole in front of the test subject's nose and mouth area to accommodate the nebulizer nozzle.

(3) The test subject shall don the test enclosure. Throughout the threshold screening test, the test subject shall breathe through his or her slightly open mouth with tongue extended. The subject is instructed to report when he/she detects a bitter taste

(4) Using a DeVilbiss Model 40 Inhalation Medication Nebulizer or equivalent, the test conductor shall spray the Threshold Check Solution into the enclosure. This Nebulizer shall be clearly marked to distinguish it from the fit test solution nebulizer.

(5) The Threshold Check Solution is prepared by adding 13.5 milligrams of Bitrex to 100 ml of 5% salt (NaCl) solution in distilled water.

(6) To produce the aerosol, the nebulizer bulb is firmly squeezed so that the bulb collapses completely, and is then released and allowed to fully expand.

(7) An initial ten squeezes are repeated rapidly and then the test subject is asked whether the Bitrex can be tasted. If the test subject reports tasting the bitter taste during the ten squeezes, the screening test is completed. The taste threshold is noted as ten regardless of the number of squeezes actually completed.

(8) If the first response is negative, ten more squeezes are repeated rapidly and the test subject is again asked whether the Bitrex is tasted. If the test subject reports tasting the bitter taste during the second ten squeezes, the screening test is completed. The taste threshold is noted as twenty regardless of the number of squeezes actually completed.

(9) If the second response is negative, ten more squeezes are repeated rapidly and the test subject is again asked whether the Bitrex is tasted. If the test subject reports tasting the bitter taste during the third set of ten squeezes, the screening test is completed. The taste threshold is

noted as thirty regardless of the number of squeezes actually completed.

(10) The test conductor will take note of the number of squeezes required to solicit a taste response.

(11) If the Bitrex is not tasted after 30 squeezes (step 10), the test subject is unable to taste Bitrex and may not perform the Bitrex fit test.

(12) If a taste response is elicited, the test subject shall be asked to take note of the taste for reference in the fit test.

(13) Correct use of the nebulizer means that approximately 1 ml of liquid is used at a time in the nebulizer body.

(14) The nebulizer shall be thoroughly rinsed in water, shaken to dry, and refilled at least each morning and afternoon or at least every four hours.

(b) Bitrex Solution Aerosol Fit Test Procedure.

(1) The test subject may not eat, drink (except plain water), smoke, or chew gum for 15 minutes before the test.

(2) The fit test uses the same enclosure as that described in 4. (a) above.

(3) The test subject shall don the enclosure while wearing the respirator selected according to section I. A. of this appendix. The respirator shall be properly adjusted and equipped with any type particulate filter(s).

(4) A second DeVilbiss Model 40 Inhalation Medication Nebulizer or equivalent is used to spray the fit test solution into the enclosure. This nebulizer shall be clearly marked to distinguish it from the screening test solution nebulizer.

(5) The fit test solution is prepared by adding 337.5 mg of Bitrex to 200 ml of a 5% salt (NaCl) solution in warm water.

(6) As before, the test subject shall breathe through his or her slightly open mouth with tongue extended, and be instructed to report if he/she tastes the bitter taste of Bitrex.

(7) The nebulizer is inserted into the hole in the front of the enclosure and an initial concentra-

tion of the fit test solution is sprayed into the enclosure using the same number of squeezes (either 10, 20 or 30 squeezes) based on the number of squeezes required to elicit a taste response as noted during the screening test.

(8) After generating the aerosol, the test subject shall be instructed to perform the exercises in section I. A. 14. of this appendix.

(9) Every 30 seconds the aerosol concentration shall be replenished using one half the number of squeezes used initially (e.g., 5, 10 or 15).

(10) The test subject shall indicate to the test conductor if at any time during the fit test the taste of Bitrex is detected. If the test subject does not report tasting the Bitrex, the test is passed.

(11) If the taste of Bitrex is detected, the fit is deemed unsatisfactory and the test is failed. A different respirator shall be tried and the entire test procedure is repeated (taste threshold screening and fit testing).

5. Irritant Smoke (Stannic Chloride) Protocol

This qualitative fit test uses a person's response to the irritating chemicals released in the "smoke" produced by a stannic chloride ventilation smoke tube to detect leakage into the respirator.

(a) General Requirements and Precautions

(1) The respirator to be tested shall be equipped with high efficiency particulate air (HEPA) or P100 series filter(s).

(2) Only stannic chloride smoke tubes shall be used for this protocol.

(3) No form of test enclosure or hood for the test subject shall be used.

(4) The smoke can be irritating to the eyes, lungs, and nasal passages. The test conductor shall take precautions to minimize the test subject's exposure to irritant smoke. Sensitivity varies, and certain individuals may respond to a greater degree to irritant smoke. Care shall be taken when performing the sensitivity screening checks that determine whether the test subject can detect irritant smoke to use only the minimum amount of smoke necessary to elicit a response from the test subject.

(5) The fit test shall be performed in an area with adequate ventilation to prevent exposure of the person conducting the fit test or the build-up of irritant smoke in the general atmosphere.

(b) Sensitivity Screening Check

The person to be tested must demonstrate his or her ability to detect a weak concentration of the irritant smoke.

(1) The test operator shall break both ends of a ventilation smoke tube containing stannic chloride, and attach one end of the smoke tube to a low flow air pump set to deliver 200 milliliters per minute, or an aspirator squeeze bulb. The test operator shall cover the other end of the smoke tube with a short piece of tubing to prevent potential injury from the jagged end of the smoke tube.

(2) The test operator shall advise the test subject that the smoke can be irritating to the eyes, lungs, and nasal passages and instruct the subject to keep his/her eyes closed while the test is performed.

(3) The test subject shall be allowed to smell a weak concentration of the irritant smoke before the respirator is donned to become familiar with its irritating properties and to determine if he/she can detect the irritating properties of the smoke. The test operator shall carefully direct a small amount of the irritant smoke in the test subject's direction to determine that he/she can detect it.

(c) Irritant Smoke Fit Test Procedure

(1) The person being fit tested shall don the respirator without assistance, and perform the required user seal check(s).

(2) The test subject shall be instructed to keep his/her eyes closed.

(3) The test operator shall direct the stream of irritant smoke from the smoke tube toward the faceseal area of the test subject, using the low flow pump or the squeeze bulb. The test operator shall begin at least 12 inches from the facepiece and move the smoke stream around the whole perimeter of the mask. The operator shall gradually make two more passes around the perimeter of the mask, moving to within six inches of the respirator.

(4) If the person being tested has not had an involuntary response and/or detected the irritant

smoke, proceed with the test exercises.

(5) The exercises identified in section I.A. 14. of this appendix shall be performed by the test subject while the respirator seal is being continually challenged by the smoke, directed around the perimeter of the respirator at a distance of six inches.

(6) If the person being fit tested reports detecting the irritant smoke at any time, the test is failed. The person being retested must repeat the entire sensitivity check and fit test procedure.

(7) Each test subject passing the irritant smoke test without evidence of a response (involuntary cough, irritation) shall be given a second sensitivity screening check, with the smoke from the same smoke tube used during the fit test, once the respirator has been removed, to determine whether he/she still reacts to the smoke. Failure to evoke a response shall void the fit test.

(8) If a response is produced during this second sensitivity check, then the fit test is passed.

C. Quantitative Fit Test (QNFT) Protocols

The following quantitative fit testing procedures have been demonstrated to be acceptable: Quantitative fit testing using a non-hazardous test aerosol (such as corn oil, polyethylene glycol 400 [PEG 400], di-2-ethyl hexyl sebacate [DEHS], or sodium chloride) generated in a test chamber, and employing instrumentation to quantify the fit of the respirator; Quantitative fit testing using ambient aerosol as the test agent and appropriate instrumentation (condensation nuclei counter) to quantify the respirator fit; Quantitative fit testing using controlled negative pressure and appropriate instrumentation to measure the volumetric leak rate of a facepiece to quantify the respirator fit.

1. General

(a) The employer shall ensure that persons administering QNFT are able to calibrate equipment and perform tests properly, recognize invalid tests, calculate fit factors properly and ensure that test equipment is in proper working order.

(b) The employer shall ensure that QNFT equipment is kept clean, and is maintained and calibrated according to the manufacturer's instructions so as to operate at the parameters for which it was designed.

2. Generated Aerosol Quantitative Fit Testing Protocol

(a) Apparatus.

(1) Instrumentation. Aerosol generation, dilution, and measurement systems using particulates (corn oil, polyethylene glycol 400 [PEG 400], di-2-ethyl hexyl sebacate [DEHS] or sodium chloride) as test aerosols shall be used for quantitative fit testing.

(2) Test chamber. The test chamber shall be large enough to permit all test subjects to perform freely all required exercises without disturbing the test agent concentration or the measurement apparatus. The test chamber shall be equipped and constructed so that the test agent is effectively isolated from the ambient air, yet uniform in concentration throughout the chamber.

(3) When testing air-purifying respirators, the normal filter or cartridge element shall be replaced with a high efficiency particulate air (HEPA) or P100 series filter supplied by the same manufacturer.

(4) The sampling instrument shall be selected so that a computer record or strip chart record may be made of the test showing the rise and fall of the test agent concentration with each inspiration and expiration at fit factors of at least 2,000. Integrators or computers that integrate the amount of test agent penetration leakage into the respirator for each exercise may be used provided a record of the readings is made.

(5) The combination of substitute air-purifying elements, test agent and test agent concentration shall be such that the test subject is not exposed in excess of an established exposure limit for the test agent at any time during the testing process, based upon the length of the exposure and the exposure limit duration.

(6) The sampling port on the test specimen respirator shall be placed and constructed so that no leakage occurs around the port (e.g., where the respirator is probed), a free air flow is allowed into the sampling line at all times, and there is no interference with the fit or performance of the respirator. The in-mask sampling device (probe) shall be designed and used so that the air sample is drawn from the breathing zone of the test subject, midway between the nose and mouth and with the probe extending into the facepiece cavity at least 1/4 inch.

(7) The test setup shall permit the person administering the test to observe the test subject inside the chamber during the test.

(8) The equipment generating the test atmosphere shall maintain the concentration of test agent constant to within a 10 percent variation for the duration of the test.

(9) The time lag (interval between an event and the recording of the event on the strip chart or computer or integrator) shall be kept to a minimum. There shall be a clear association between the occurrence of an event and its being recorded.

(10) The sampling line tubing for the test chamber atmosphere and for the respirator sampling port shall be of equal diameter and of the same material. The length of the two lines shall be equal.

(11) The exhaust flow from the test chamber shall pass through an appropriate filter (i.e., high efficiency particulate filter) before release.

(12) When sodium chloride aerosol is used, the relative humidity inside the test chamber shall not exceed 50 percent.

(13) The limitations of instrument detection shall be taken into account when determining the fit factor.

(14) Test respirators shall be maintained in proper working order and be inspected regularly for deficiencies such as cracks or missing valves and gaskets.

(b) Procedural Requirements.

(1) When performing the initial user seal check using a positive or negative pressure check, the sampling line shall be crimped closed in order to avoid air pressure leakage during either of these pressure checks.

(2) The use of an abbreviated screening QLFT test is optional. Such a test may be utilized in order to quickly identify poor fitting respirators that passed the positive and/or negative pressure test and reduce the amount of QNFT time. The use of the CNC QNFT instrument in the count mode is another optional method to obtain a quick estimate of fit and eliminate poor fitting respirators before going on to perform a full QNFT.

(3) A reasonably stable test agent concentration shall be measured in the test chamber prior to testing. For canopy or shower curtain types of test units, the determination of the test agent's stability may be established after the test subject has entered the test environment.

(4) Immediately after the subject enters the test chamber, the test agent concentration inside the respirator shall be measured to ensure that the peak penetration does not exceed 5 percent for a half mask or 1 percent for a full facepiece respirator.

(5) A stable test agent concentration shall be obtained prior to the actual start of testing.

(6) Respirator restraining straps shall not be over-tightened for testing. The straps shall be adjusted by the wearer without assistance from other persons to give a reasonably comfortable fit typical of normal use. The respirator shall not be adjusted once the fit test exercises begin.

(7) The test shall be terminated whenever any single peak penetration exceeds 5 percent for half masks and 1 percent for full facepiece respirators. The test subject shall be refitted and retested.

(8) Calculation of fit factors.

(i) The fit factor shall be determined for the quantitative fit test by taking the ratio of the average chamber concentration to the concentration measured inside the respirator for each test exercise except the grimace exercise.

(ii) The average test chamber concentration shall be calculated as the arithmetic average of the concentration measured before and after each test (i.e., 7 exercises) or the arithmetic average of the concentration measured before and after each exercise or the true average measured continuously during the respirator sample.

(iii) The concentration of the challenge agent inside the respirator shall be determined by one of the following methods:

(A) Average peak penetration method means the method of determining test agent penetration into the respirator utilizing a strip chart recorder, integrator, or computer. The agent

penetration is determined by an average of the peak heights on the graph or by computer integration, for each exercise except the grimace exercise. Integrators or computers that calculate the actual test agent penetration into the respirator for each exercise will also be considered to meet the requirements of the average peak penetration method.

(B) Maximum peak penetration method means the method of determining test agent penetration in the respirator as determined by strip chart recordings of the test. The highest peak penetration for a given exercise is taken to be representative of average penetration into the respirator for that exercise.

(C) Integration by calculation of the area under the individual peak for each exercise except the grimace exercise. This includes computerized integration.

(D) The calculation of the overall fit factor using individual exercise fit factors involves first converting the exercise fit factors to penetration values, determining the average, and then converting that result back to a fit factor. This procedure is described in the following equation:

$$\text{Overall Fit Factor} = \frac{\text{Number of exercises}}{1/ff_1 + 1/ff_2 + 1/ff_3 + 1/ff_4 + 1/ff_5 + 1/ff_6 + 1/ff_7 + 1/ff_8}$$

Where ff_1, ff_2, ff_3, etc. are the fit factors for exercises 1, 2, 3, etc.

(9) The test subject shall not be permitted to wear a half mask or quarter facepiece respirator unless a minimum fit factor of 100 is obtained, or a full facepiece respirator unless a minimum fit factor of 500 is obtained.

(10) Filters used for quantitative fit testing shall be replaced whenever increased breathing resistance is encountered, or when the test agent has altered the integrity of the filter media.

3. Ambient aerosol condensation nuclei counter (CNC) quantitative fit testing protocol.

The ambient aerosol condensation nuclei counter (CNC) quantitative fit testing (Portacount ™) protocol quantitatively fit tests respirators with the use of a probe. The probed respirator is only used for quantitative fit tests. A probed respirator has a special sampling device, installed on the respirator, that allows the probe to sample the air from inside the mask. A probed respirator is required for each make, style, model, and size that the employer uses and can be obtained from the respirator manufacturer or distributor. The CNC instrument manufacturer, TSI Inc., also provides probe attachments (TSI sampling adapters) that permit fit testing in an employee's own respirator. A minimum fit factor pass level of at least 100 is necessary for a half-mask respirator and a minimum fit factor pass level of at least 500 is required for a full facepiece negative pressure respirator. The entire screening and testing procedure shall be explained to the test subject prior to the conduct of the screening test.

(a) Portacount Fit Test Requirements.

(1) Check the respirator to make sure the sampling probe and line are properly attached to the facepiece and that the respirator is fitted with a particulate filter capable of preventing significant penetration by the ambient particles used for the fit test (e.g., NIOSH 42 CFR 84 series 100, series 99, or series 95 particulate filter) per manufacturer's instruction.

(2) Instruct the person to be tested to don the respirator for five minutes before the fit test starts. This purges the ambient particles trapped inside the respirator and permits the wearer to make certain the respirator is comfortable. This individual shall already have been trained on how to wear the respirator properly.

(3) Check the following conditions for the adequacy of the respirator fit: Chin properly placed; Adequate strap tension, not overly tightened; Fit across nose bridge; Respirator of proper size to span distance from nose to chin; Tendency of the respirator to slip; Self-observation in a mirror to evaluate fit and respirator position.

(4) Have the person wearing the respirator do a user seal check. If leakage is detected, determine the cause. If leakage is from a poorly fitting facepiece, try another size of the same model respirator, or another model of respirator.

(5) Follow the manufacturer's instructions for operating the Portacount and proceed with the test.

(6) The test subject shall be instructed to perform the exercises in section I. A. 14. of this appendix.

(7) After the test exercises, the test subject shall be questioned by the test conductor regarding

the comfort of the respirator upon completion of the protocol. If it has become unacceptable, another model of respirator shall be tried.

(b) Portacount Test Instrument.

(1) The Portacount will automatically stop and calculate the overall fit factor for the entire set of exercises. The overall fit factor is what counts. The Pass or Fail message will indicate whether or not the test was successful. If the test was a Pass, the fit test is over.

(2) Since the pass or fail criterion of the Portacount is user programmable, the test operator shall ensure that the pass or fail criterion meet the requirements for minimum respirator performance in this Appendix.

(3) A record of the test needs to be kept on file, assuming the fit test was successful. The record must contain the test subject's name; overall fit factor; make, model, style, and size of respirator used; and date tested.

4. Controlled negative pressure (CNP) quantitative fit testing protocol.

The CNP protocol provides an alternative to aerosol fit test methods. The CNP fit test method technology is based on exhausting air from a temporarily sealed respirator facepiece to generate and then maintain a constant negative pressure inside the facepiece. The rate of air exhaust is controlled so that a constant negative pressure is maintained in the respirator during the fit test. The level of pressure is selected to replicate the mean inspiratory pressure that causes leakage into the respirator under normal use conditions. With pressure held constant, air flow out of the respirator is equal to air flow into the respirator. Therefore, measurement of the exhaust stream that is required to hold the pressure in the temporarily sealed respirator constant yields a direct measure of leakage air flow into the respirator. The CNP fit test method measures leak rates through the facepiece as a method for determining the facepiece fit for negative pressure respirators. The CNP instrument manufacturer Occupational Health Dynamics of Birmingham, Alabama also provides attachments (sampling manifolds) that replace the filter cartridges to permit fit testing in an employee's own respirator. To perform the test, the test subject closes his or her mouth and holds his/her breath, after which an air pump removes air from the respirator facepiece at a pre-selected constant pressure. The facepiece fit is expressed as the leak rate through the facepiece, ex-

pressed as milliliters per minute. The quality and validity of the CNP fit tests are determined by the degree to which the in-mask pressure tracks the test pressure during the system measurement time of approximately five seconds. Instantaneous feedback in the form of a real-time pressure trace of the in-mask pressure is provided and used to determine test validity and quality. A minimum fit factor pass level of 100 is necessary for a half-mask respirator and a minimum fit factor of at least 500 is required for a full facepiece respirator. The entire screening and testing procedure shall be explained to the test subject prior to the conduct of the screening test.

(a) CNP Fit Test Requirements.

(1) The instrument shall have a non-adjustable test pressure of 15.0 mm water pressure.

(2) The CNP system defaults selected for test pressure shall be set at -- 15 mm of water (-0.58 inches of water) and the modeled inspiratory flow rate shall be 53.8 liters per minute for performing fit tests.

(Note: CNP systems have built-in capability to conduct fit testing that is specific to unique work rate, mask, and gender situations that might apply in a specific workplace. Use of system default values, which were selected to represent respirator wear with medium cartridge resistance at a low-moderate work rate, will allow inter-test comparison of the respirator fit.)

(3) The individual who conducts the CNP fit testing shall be thoroughly trained to perform the test.

(4) The respirator filter or cartridge needs to be replaced with the CNP test manifold. The inhalation valve downstream from the manifold either needs to be temporarily removed or propped open.

(5) The employer must train the test subject to hold his or her breath for at least 10 seconds.

(6) The test subject must don the test respirator without any assistance from the test administrator who is conducting the CNP fit test. The respirator must not be adjusted once the fit-test exercises begin. Any adjustment voids the test, and the test subject must repeat the fit test.

(7) The QNFT protocol shall be followed according to section I. C. 1. of this appendix with an exception for the CNP test exercises.

(b) CNP Test Exercises.

(1) Normal breathing. In a normal standing position, without talking, the subject shall breathe normally for 1 minute. After the normal breathing exercise, the subject needs to hold head straight ahead and hold his or her breath for 10 seconds during the test measurement.

(2) Deep breathing. In a normal standing position, the subject shall breathe slowly and deeply for 1 minute, being careful not to hyperventilate. After the deep breathing exercise, the subject shall hold his or her head straight ahead and hold his or her breath for 10 seconds during test measurement.

(3) Turning head side to side. Standing in place, the subject shall slowly turn his or her head from side to side between the extreme positions on each side for 1 minute. The head shall be held at each extreme momentarily so the subject can inhale at each side. After the turning head side to side exercise, the subject needs to hold head full left and hold his or her breath for 10 seconds during test measurement. Next, the subject needs to hold head full right and hold his or her breath for 10 seconds during test measurement.

(4) Moving head up and down. Standing in place, the subject shall slowly move his or her head up and down for 1 minute. The subject shall be instructed to inhale in the up position (i.e., when looking toward the ceiling). After the moving head up and down exercise, the subject shall hold his or her head full up and hold his or her breath for 10 seconds during test measurement. Next, the subject shall hold his or her head full down and hold his or her breath for 10 seconds during test measurement.

(5) Talking. The subject shall talk out loud slowly and loud enough so as to be heard clearly by the test conductor. The subject can read from a prepared text such as the Rainbow Passage, count backward from 100, or recite a memorized poem or song for 1 minute. After the talking exercise, the subject shall hold his or her head straight ahead and hold his or her breath for 10 seconds during the test measurement.

(6) Grimace. The test subject shall grimace by smiling or frowning for 15 seconds.

(7) Bending Over. The test subject shall bend at the waist as if he or she were to touch his or her toes for 1 minute. Jogging in place shall be sub-stituted for this exercise in those test environments such as shroud-type QNFT units that prohibit bending at the waist. After the bending over exercise, the subject shall hold his or her head straight ahead and hold his or her breath for 10 seconds during the test measurement.

(8) Normal Breathing. The test subject shall remove and re-don the respirator within a one-minute period. Then, in a normal standing position, without talking, the subject shall breathe normally for 1 minute. After the normal breathing exercise, the subject shall hold his or her head straight ahead and hold his or her breath for 10 seconds during the test measurement. After the test exercises, the test subject shall be questioned by the test conductor regarding the comfort of the respirator upon completion of the protocol. If it has become unacceptable, another model of a respirator shall be tried.

(c) CNP Test Instrument.

(1) The test instrument must have an effective audio-warning device, or a visual-warning device in the form of a screen tracing, that indicates when the test subject fails to hold his or her breath during the test. The test must be terminated and restarted from the beginning when the test subject fails to hold his or her breath during the test. The test subject then may be re-fitted and retested.

(2) A record of the test shall be kept on file, assuming the fit test was successful. The record must contain the test subject's name; overall fit factor; make, model, style and size of respirator used; and date tested.

5. Controlled negative pressure (CNP) REDON quantitative fit testing protocol.

(a) When administering this protocol to test subjects, employers must comply with the requirements specified in paragraphs (a) and (c) of Part I.C.4 of this appendix ("Controlled negative pressure (CNP) quantitative fit testing protocol"), as well as use the test exercises described below in paragraph (b) of this protocol instead of the test exercises specified in paragraph (b) of Part I.C.4 of this appendix.

(b) Employers must ensure that each test subject being fit tested using this protocol follows the exercise and measurement procedures, including the order of administration, described below in Table A-1 of this appendix.

Table A-1. CNP REDON Quantitative Fit Testing Protocol

Exercises(1)	Exercise procedure	Measurement procedure
Facing Forward	Stand and breathe normally, without talking, for 30 seconds.	Face forward, while holding breath for 10 seconds.
Bending Over	Bend at the waist, as if going to touch his or her toes, for 30 seconds.	Face parallel to the floor, while holding breath for 10 seconds
Head Shaking	For about three seconds, shake head back and forth vigorously several times while shouting.	Face forward, while holding breath for 10 seconds.
REDON 1	Remove the respirator mask, loosen all facepiece straps, and then redon the respirator mask.	Face forward, while holding breath for 10 seconds.
REDON 2	Remove the respirator mask, loosen all facepiece straps, and then redon the respirator mask again.	Face forward, while holding breath for 10 seconds.

[1] Exercises are listed in the order in which they are to be administered.

(c) After completing the test exercises, the test administrator must question each test subject regarding the comfort of the respirator. When a test subject states that the respirator is unacceptable, the employer must ensure that the test administrator repeats the protocol using another respirator model.

(d) Employers must determine the overall fit factor for each test subject by calculating the harmonic mean of the fit testing exercises as follows:

$$\text{Overall Fit Factor} = \frac{N}{[1/FF_1 + 1/FF_2 + ... 1/FF_N]}$$

Where:
N = The number of exercises;
FF_1 = The fit factor for the first exercise;
FF_2 = The fit factor for the second exercise; and
FF_N = The fit factor for the nth exercise.

Part II. New Fit Test Protocols

A. Any person may submit to OSHA an application for approval of a new fit test protocol. If the application meets the following criteria, OSHA will initiate a rulemaking proceeding under section 6(b)(7) of the OSH Act to determine whether to list the new protocol as an approved protocol in this Appendix A.

B. The application must include a detailed description of the proposed new fit test protocol. This application must be supported by either:

1. A test report prepared by an independent government research laboratory (e.g., Lawrence Livermore National Laboratory, Los Alamos National Laboratory, the National Institute for Standards and Technology) stating that the laboratory has tested the protocol and had found it to be accurate and reliable; or

2. An article that has been published in a peer-reviewed industrial hygiene journal describing the protocol and explaining how test data support the protocol's accuracy and reliability.

C. If OSHA determines that additional information is required before the Agency commences a rulemaking proceeding under this section, OSHA will so notify the applicant and afford the applicant the opportunity to submit the supplemental information. Initiation of a rulemaking proceeding will be deferred until OSHA has received and evaluated the supplemental information.

Appendix B-1 to §1910.134: User Seal Check Procedures (Mandatory)

The individual who uses a tight-fitting respirator is to perform a user seal check to ensure that an adequate seal is achieved each time the respirator is put on. Either the positive and negative pressure checks listed in this appendix, or the respirator manufacturer's recommended user seal check method shall be used. User seal checks are not substitutes for qualitative or quantitative fit tests.

I. Facepiece Positive and/or Negative Pressure Checks

A. Positive pressure check. Close off the exhalation valve and exhale gently into the facepiece. The face fit is considered satisfactory if a slight positive pressure can be built up inside the facepiece without any evidence of outward leakage of air at the seal. For most respirators this method of leak testing requires the wearer to first remove the exhalation valve cover before closing off the exhalation valve and then carefully replacing it after the test.

B. Negative pressure check. Close off the inlet opening of the canister or cartridge(s) by covering with the palm of the hand(s) or by replacing the filter seal(s), inhale gently so that the facepiece collapses slightly, and hold the breath for ten seconds. The design of the inlet opening of some cartridges cannot be effectively covered with the palm of the hand. The test can be performed by covering the inlet opening of the cartridge with a thin latex or nitrile glove. If the facepiece remains in its slightly collapsed condition and no inward leakage of air is detected, the tightness of the respirator is considered satisfactory.

II. Manufacturer's Recommended User Seal Check Procedures

The respirator manufacturer's recommended procedures for performing a user seal check may be used instead of the positive and/or negative pressure check procedures provided that the employer demonstrates that the manufacturer's procedures are equally effective.

Appendix B-2 to §1910.134: Respirator Cleaning Procedures (Mandatory)

These procedures are provided for employer use when cleaning respirators. They are general in nature, and the employer as an alternative may use the cleaning recommendations provided by the manufacturer of the respirators used by their employees, provided such procedures are as effective as those listed here in Appendix B- 2. Equivalent effectiveness simply means that the procedures used must accomplish the objectives set forth in Appendix B-2, i.e., must ensure that the respirator is properly cleaned and disinfected in a manner that prevents damage to the respirator and does not cause harm to the user.

I. Procedures for Cleaning Respirators

A. Remove filters, cartridges, or canisters. Disassemble facepieces by removing speaking diaphragms, demand and pressure-demand valve assemblies, hoses, or any components recommended by the manufacturer. Discard or repair any defective parts.

B. Wash components in warm (43 deg. C [110 deg. F] maximum) water with a mild detergent or with a cleaner recommended by the manufacturer. A stiff bristle (not wire) brush may be used to facilitate the removal of dirt.

C. Rinse components thoroughly in clean, warm (43 deg. C [110 deg. F] maximum), preferably running water. Drain.

D. When the cleaner used does not contain a disinfecting agent, respirator components should be immersed for two minutes in one of the following:

1. Hypochlorite solution (50 ppm of chlorine) made by adding approximately one milliliter of laundry bleach to one liter of water at 43 deg. C (110 deg. F); or,

2. Aqueous solution of iodine (50 ppm iodine) made by adding approximately 0.8 milliliters of tincture of iodine (6-8 grams ammonium and/or potassium iodide/100 cc of 45% alcohol) to one liter of water at 43 deg. C (110 deg. F); or,

3. Other commercially available cleansers of equivalent disinfectant quality when used as directed, if their use is recommended or approved by the respirator manufacturer.

E. Rinse components thoroughly in clean, warm (43 deg. C [110 deg. F] maximum), preferably running water. Drain. The importance of thorough rinsing cannot be overemphasized. Detergents or disinfectants that dry on facepieces may result in dermatitis. In addition, some disinfectants may cause deterioration of rubber or corrosion of metal parts if not completely removed.

F. Components should be hand-dried with a clean lint-free cloth or air-dried.

G. Reassemble facepiece, replacing filters, cartridges, and canisters where necessary.

H. Test the respirator to ensure that all components work properly.

Appendix C to §1910.134: OSHA Respirator Medical Evaluation Questionnaire (Mandatory)

To the employer: Answers to questions in Section 1, and to question 9 in Section 2 of Part A, do not require a medical examination.

To the employee:

Can you read (circle one): Yes/No

Your employer must allow you to answer this questionnaire during normal working hours, or at a time and place that is convenient to you. To maintain your confidentiality, your employer or supervisor must not look at or review your answers, and your employer must tell you how to deliver or send this questionnaire to the health care professional who will review it.

Part A. Section 1. (Mandatory)

The following information must be provided by every employee who has been selected to use any type of respirator (please print).

1. Today's date:_____

2. Your name:_____

3. Your age (to nearest year):_____

4. Sex (circle one): Male/Female

5. Your height: _____ ft. _____ in.

6. Your weight: _____ lbs.

7. Your job title:_____

8. A phone number where you can be reached by the health care professional who reviews this questionnaire (include the Area Code): _____

9. The best time to phone you at this number:

_____

10. Has your employer told you how to contact the health care professional who will review this questionnaire (circle one): Yes/No

11. Check the type of respirator you will use (you can check more than one category):

a. _____ N, R, or P disposable respirator (filter-mask, non-cartridge type only).

b. _____ Other type (for example, half- or full-face-piece type, powered-air purifying, supplied-air, self-contained breathing apparatus).

12. Have you worn a respirator (circle one): Yes/No

If "yes," what type(s):_____

_____

_____

Part A. Section 2. (Mandatory)

Questions 1 through 9 below must be answered by every employee who has been selected to use any type of respirator (please circle "yes" or "no").

1. Do you **currently** smoke tobacco, or have you smoked tobacco in the last month: Yes/No

2. Have you **ever had** any of the following conditions?

Seizures (fits): Yes/No

Diabetes (sugar disease): Yes/No

Allergic reactions that interfere with your breathing: Yes/No

Claustrophobia (fear of closed-in places): Yes/No

Trouble smelling odors: Yes/No

3. Have you **ever had** any of the following pulmonary or lung problems?

Asbestosis: Yes/No

Asthma: Yes/No

Chronic bronchitis: Yes/No

Emphysema: Yes/No

Pneumonia: Yes/No

Tuberculosis: Yes/No

Silicosis: Yes/No

Pneumothorax (collapsed lung): Yes/No

Lung cancer: Yes/No

Broken ribs: Yes/No

Any chest injuries or surgeries: Yes/No

Any other lung problem that you've been told about: Yes/No

4. Do you **currently** have any of the following symptoms of pulmonary or lung illness?

Shortness of breath: Yes/No

Shortness of breath when walking fast on level ground or walking up a slight hill or incline: Yes/No

Shortness of breath when walking with other people at an ordinary pace on level ground: Yes/No

Have to stop for breath when walking at your own pace on level ground: Yes/No

Shortness of breath when washing or dressing yourself: Yes/No

Shortness of breath that interferes with your job: Yes/No

Coughing that produces phlegm (thick sputum): Yes/No

Coughing that wakes you early in the morning: Yes/No

Coughing that occurs mostly when you are lying down: Yes/No

Coughing up blood in the last month: Yes/No

Wheezing: Yes/No

Wheezing that interferes with your job: Yes/No

Chest pain when you breathe deeply: Yes/No

Any other symptoms that you think may be related to lung problems: Yes/No

5. Have you **ever had** any of the following cardiovascular or heart problems?

Heart attack: Yes/No

Stroke: Yes/No

Angina: Yes/No

Heart failure: Yes/No

Swelling in your legs or feet (not caused by walking): Yes/No

Heart arrhythmia (heart beating irregularly): Yes/No

High blood pressure: Yes/No

Any other heart problem that you've been told about: Yes/No

6. Have you **ever had** any of the following cardiovascular or heart symptoms?

Frequent pain or tightness in your chest: Yes/No

Pain or tightness in your chest during physical activity: Yes/No

Pain or tightness in your chest that interferes with your job: Yes/No

In the past two years, have you noticed your heart skipping or missing a beat: Yes/No

Heartburn or indigestion that is not related to eating: Yes/ No

Any other symptoms that you think may be related to heart or circulation problems: Yes/No

7. Do you **currently** take medication for any of the following problems?

Breathing or lung problems: Yes/No

Heart trouble: Yes/No

Blood pressure: Yes/No

Seizures (fits): Yes/No

8. If you've used a respirator, have you **ever had** any of the following problems? (If you've never used a respirator, check the following space and go to question 9:)

Eye irritation: Yes/No

Skin allergies or rashes: Yes/No

Anxiety: Yes/No

General weakness or fatigue: Yes/No

Any other problem that interferes with your use of a respirator: Yes/No

9. Would you like to talk to the health care professional who will review this questionnaire about your answers to this questionnaire: Yes/No

Questions 10 to 15 below must be answered by every employee who has been selected to use either a full-facepiece respirator or a self-contained breathing apparatus (SCBA). For employees who have been selected to use other types of respirators, answering these questions is voluntary.

10. Have you **ever lost** vision in either eye (temporarily or permanently): Yes/No

11. Do you **currently** have any of the following vision problems?

Wear contact lenses: Yes/No

Wear glasses: Yes/No

Color blind: Yes/No

Any other eye or vision problem: Yes/No

12. Have you **ever had** an injury to your ears, including a broken ear drum: Yes/No

13. Do you **currently** have any of the following hearing problems?

Difficulty hearing: Yes/No

Wear a hearing aid: Yes/No

Any other hearing or ear problem: Yes/No

14. Have you **ever had** a back injury: Yes/No

15. Do you **currently** have any of the following musculoskeletal problems?

Weakness in any of your arms, hands, legs, or feet: Yes/No

Back pain: Yes/No

Difficulty fully moving your arms and legs: Yes/No

Pain or stiffness when you lean forward or backward at the waist: Yes/No

Difficulty fully moving your head up or down: Yes/No

Difficulty fully moving your head side to side: Yes/No

Difficulty bending at your knees: Yes/No

Difficulty squatting to the ground: Yes/No

Climbing a flight of stairs or a ladder carrying more than 25 lbs: Yes/No

Any other muscle or skeletal problem that interferes with using a respirator: Yes/No

Part B

Any of the following questions, and other questions not listed, may be added to the questionnaire at the discretion of the health care professional who will review the questionnaire.

1. In your present job, are you working at high altitudes (over 5,000 feet) or in a place that has lower than normal amounts of oxygen: Yes/No

   If "yes," do you have feelings of dizziness, shortness of breath, pounding in your chest, or other symptoms when you're working under these conditions: Yes/No

2. At work or at home, have you ever been exposed to hazardous solvents, hazardous airborne chemicals (e.g., gases, fumes, or dust), or have you come into skin contact with hazardous chemicals: Yes/No

   If "yes," name the chemicals if you know them:_____
   _____
   _____
   _____

3. Have you ever worked with any of the materials, or under any of the conditions, listed below:

   Asbestos: Yes/No

   Silica (e.g., in sandblasting): Yes/No

   Tungsten/cobalt (e.g., grinding or welding this material): Yes/No

   Beryllium: Yes/No

   Aluminum: Yes/No

   Coal (for example, mining): Yes/No

   Iron: Yes/No

   Tin: Yes/No

   Dusty environments: Yes/No

   Any other hazardous exposures: Yes/No

If "yes," describe these exposures:_____
_____
_____
_____

4. List any second jobs or side businesses you have:_____
_____

5. List your previous occupations:_____
_____
_____

6. List your current and previous hobbies:_____
_____
_____

7. Have you been in the military services? Yes/No

   If "yes," were you exposed to biological or chemical agents (either in training or combat): Yes/No

8. Have you ever worked on a HAZMAT team? Yes/No

9. Other than medications for breathing and lung problems, heart trouble, blood pressure, and seizures mentioned earlier in this questionnaire, are you taking any other medications for any reason (including over-the-counter medications): Yes/No

   If "yes," name the medications if you know them:_____

10. Will you be using any of the following items with your respirator(s)?
    HEPA Filters: Yes/No
    Canisters (for example, gas masks): Yes/No
    Cartridges: Yes/No

11. How often are you expected to use the respirator(s) (circle "yes" or "no" for all answers that apply to you)?:
    Escape only (no rescue): Yes/No
    Emergency rescue only: Yes/No
    Less than 5 hours **per week**: Yes/No
    Less than 2 hours **per day**: Yes/No
    2 to 4 hours per day: Yes/No
    Over 4 hours per day: Yes/No

12. During the period you are using the respirator(s), is your work effort:
    Light (less than 200 kcal per hour): Yes/No

    If "yes," how long does this period last during the average shift:_____hrs._____mins.

    Examples of a light work effort are **sitting** while

writing, typing, drafting, or performing light assembly work; or **standing** while operating a drill press (1-3 lbs.) or controlling machines.

Moderate (200 to 350 kcal per hour): Yes/No

If "yes," how long does this period last during the average shift:_____hrs._____mins.

Examples of moderate work effort are **sitting** while nailing or filing; **driving** a truck or bus in urban traffic; standing while drilling, nailing, performing assembly work, or transferring a moderate load (about 35 lbs.) at trunk level; **walking** on a level surface about 2 mph or down a 5-degree grade about 3 mph; or **pushing** a wheelbarrow with a heavy load (about 100 lbs.) on a level surface.

Heavy (above 350 kcal per hour): Yes/No

If "yes," how long does this period last during the average shift:_____hrs._____mins.

Examples of heavy work are **lifting** a heavy load (about 50 lbs.) from the floor to your waist or shoulder; working on a loading dock; **shoveling**; **standing** while bricklaying or chipping castings; **walking** up an 8-degree grade about 2 mph; climbing stairs with a heavy load (about 50 lbs.).

13. Will you be wearing protective clothing and/or equipment (other than the respirator) when you're using your respirator: Yes/No

If "yes," describe this protective clothing and/or equipment:_____

_____

14. Will you be working under hot conditions (temperature exceeding 77 deg. F): Yes/No

15. Will you be working under humid conditions: Yes/No

16. Describe the work you'll be doing while you're using your respirator(s)_____

_____

_____

17. Describe any special or hazardous conditions you might encounter when you're using your respirator(s) (for example, confined spaces, life-threatening gases):_____

_____

_____

_____

18. Provide the following information, if you know it, for each toxic substance that you'll be exposed to when you're using your respirator(s):

Name of the first toxic sustance:_____

_____

Estimated maximum exposure level per shift:_____

Duration of exposure per shift:_____

Name of the second toxic substance:_____

Estimated maximum exposure level per shift:_____

Duration of exposure per shift:_____

Name of the third toxic substance:_____

Estimated maximum exposure level per shift:_____

Duration of exposure per shift:_____

The name of any other toxic substances that you'll be exposed to while using your respirator:

_____

_____

_____

_____

_____

_____

19. Describe any special responsibilities you'll have while using your respirator(s) that may affect the safety and well-being of others (for example, rescue, security):

_____

_____

_____

_____

www.osha.gov
**Occupational Safety and
Health Administration**

Appendix D to §1910.134: Information for Employees Using Respirators When Not Required Under the Standard (Mandatory)

Respirators are an effective method of protection against designated hazards when properly selected and worn. Respirator use is encouraged, even when exposures are below the exposure limit, to provide an additional level of comfort and protection for workers. However, if a respirator is used improperly or not kept clean, the respirator itself can become a hazard to the worker. Sometimes, workers may wear respirators to avoid exposures to hazards, even if the amount of hazardous substance does not exceed the limits set by OSHA standards. If your employer provides respirators for your voluntary use, or if you provide your own respirator, you need to take certain precautions to be sure that the respirator itself does not present a hazard.

You should do the following:

1. Read and heed all instructions provided by the manufacturer on use, maintenance, cleaning and care, and warnings regarding the respirators limitations.

2. Choose respirators certified for use to protect against the contaminant of concern. NIOSH, the National Institute for Occupational Safety and Health of the U.S. Department of Health and Human Services, certifies respirators. A label or statement of certification should appear on the respirator or respirator packaging. It will tell you what the respirator is designed for and how much it will protect you.

3. Do not wear your respirator into atmospheres containing contaminants for which your respirator is not designed to protect against. For example, a respirator designed to filter dust particles will not protect you against gases, vapors, or very small solid particles of fumes or smoke.

4. Keep track of your respirator so that you do not mistakenly use someone else's respirator.

[63 FR 1152, Jan. 8, 1998; 63 FR 20098, 20099, April 23, 1998; assembled at 69 FR 46993, Aug. 4, 2004, 71 FR 16672, April 3, 2006; 71 FR 50187, August 24, 2006]

OSHA Assistance

OSHA can provide extensive help through a variety of programs, including technical assistance about effective safety and health programs, state plans, workplace consultations, voluntary protection programs, strategic partnerships, training and education, and more. An overall commitment to workplace safety and health can add value to your business, to your workplace, and to your life.

Safety and Health Program Management Guidelines

Effective management of employee safety and health protection is a decisive factor in reducing the extent and severity of work-related injuries and illnesses and their related costs. In fact, an effective safety and health program forms the basis of good employee protection, can save time and money, increase productivity and reduce employee injuries, illnesses, and related workers' compensation costs.

To assist employers and employees in developing effective safety and health programs, OSHA published recommended Safety and Health Program Management Guidelines (54 *Federal Register* (16): 3904-3916, January 26, 1989). These voluntary guidelines can be applied to all places of employment covered by OSHA.

The guidelines identify four general elements critical to the development of a successful safety and health management system:

- Management leadership and employee involvement,

- Worksite analysis,

- Hazard prevention and control, and

- Safety and health training.

The guidelines recommend specific actions, under each of these general elements, to achieve an effective safety and health program. The *Federal Register* notice is available online at www.osha.gov.

State Programs

The Occupational Safety and Health Act of 1970 (OSH Act) encourages states to develop and operate their own job safety and health plans. OSHA approves and monitors these plans. Twenty-four states, Puerto Rico, and the Virgin Islands currently operate approved state plans: 22 cover both private and public (state and local government) employment; Connecticut, New Jersey, New York, and the Virgin Islands cover the public sector only. States and territories with their own OSHA-approved occupational safety and health plans must adopt standards identi-

cal to, or at least as effective as, the Federal OSHA standards.

Consultation Services

Consultation assistance is available on request to employers who want help in establishing and maintaining a safe and healthful workplace. Largely funded by OSHA, the service is provided at no cost to the employer. Primarily developed for smaller employers with more hazardous operations, the consultation service is delivered by state governments employing professional safety and health consultants. Comprehensive assistance includes an appraisal of all mechanical systems, work practices, and occupational safety and health hazards of the workplace and all aspects of the employer's present job safety and health program. In addition, the service offers assistance to employers in developing and implementing an effective safety and health program. No penalties are proposed or citations issued for hazards identified by the consultant. OSHA provides consultation assistance to the employer with the assurance that his or her name and firm and any information about the workplace will not be routinely reported to OSHA enforcement staff.

Under the consultation program, certain exemplary employers may request participation in OSHA's Safety and Health Achievement Recognition Program (SHARP). Eligibility for participation in SHARP includes receiving a comprehensive consultation visit, demonstrating exemplary achievements in workplace safety and health by abating all identified hazards, and developing an excellent safety and health program.

Employers accepted into SHARP may receive an exemption from programmed inspections (not complaint or accident investigation inspections) for a period of 1 year. For more information concerning consultation assistance, see OSHA's website at www.osha.gov.

Voluntary Protection Programs (VPP)

Voluntary Protection Programs and on-site consultation services, when coupled with an effective enforcement program, expand employee protection to help meet the goals of the OSH Act. The VPPs motivate others to achieve excellent safety and health results in the same outstanding way as they establish a cooperative relationship between employers, employees, and OSHA.

For additional information on VPP and how to apply, contact the OSHA regional offices listed at the end of this publication.

www.osha.gov
Occupational Safety and
Health Administration

Strategic Partnership Program

OSHA's Strategic Partnership Program, the newest member of OSHA's cooperative programs, helps encourage, assist, and recognize the efforts of partners to eliminate serious workplace hazards and achieve a high level of employee safety and health. Whereas OSHA's Consultation Program and VPP entail one-on-one relationships between OSHA and individual worksites, most strategic partnerships seek to have a broader impact by building cooperative relationships with groups of employers and employees. These partnerships are voluntary, cooperative relationships between OSHA, employers, employee representatives, and others (e.g., trade unions, trade and professional associations, universities, and other government agencies).

For more information on this and other cooperative programs, contact your nearest OSHA office, or visit OSHA's website at www.osha.gov.

Alliance Program

Through the Alliance Program, OSHA works with groups committed to safety and health, including businesses, trade or professional organizations, unions and educational institutions, to leverage resources and expertise to develop compliance assistance tools and resources and share information with employers and employees to help prevent injuries, illnesses and fatalities in the workplace.

Alliance program agreements have been established with a wide variety of industries including meat, apparel, poultry, steel, plastics, maritime, printing, chemical, construction, paper and telecommunications. These agreements are addressing many safety and health hazards and at-risk audiences, including silica, fall protection, amputations, immigrant workers, youth and small businesses. By meeting the goals of the Alliance Program agreements (training and education, outreach and communication, and promoting the national dialogue on workplace safety and health), OSHA and the Alliance Program participants are developing and disseminating compliance assistance information and resources for employers and employees such as electronic assistance tools, fact sheets, toolbox talks, and training programs.

OSHA Training and Education

OSHA area offices offer a variety of information services, such as compliance assistance, technical advice, publications, audiovisual aids, and speakers for special engagements. OSHA's Training Institute in Arlington Heights, IL, provides basic and advanced courses in safety and health for Federal and state compliance officers, state consultants, Federal agency personnel, and private sector employers, employees, and their representatives.

The OSHA Training Institute also has established OSHA Training Institute Education Centers to address the increased demand for its courses from the private sector and from other federal agencies. These centers include colleges, universities, and nonprofit training organizations that have been selected after a competition for participation in the program.

OSHA also provides funds to nonprofit organizations, through grants, to conduct workplace training and education in subjects where OSHA believes there is a lack of workplace training. Grants are awarded annually. Grant recipients are expected to contribute 20 percent of the total grant cost.

For more information on training and education, contact the OSHA Training Institute, Directorate of Training and Education, 2020 South Arlington Heights Road, Arlington Heights, IL, 60005, (847) 297-4810, or see Training on OSHA's website at www.osha.gov. For further information on any OSHA program, contact your nearest OSHA regional office listed at the end of this publication.

Information Available Electronically

OSHA has a variety of materials and tools available on its website at www.osha.gov. These include electronic compliance assistance tools, such as *Safety and Health Topics Pages, eTools, Expert Advisors*; regulations, directives, publications and videos; and other information for employers and employees. OSHA's software programs and compliance assistance tools walk you through challenging safety and health issues and common problems to find the best solutions for your workplace.

A wide variety of OSHA materials, including standards, interpretations, directives, and more can be purchased on CD-ROM from the U.S. Government Printing Office, Superintendent of Documents, toll-free phone (866) 512-1800.

OSHA Publications

OSHA has an extensive publications program. For a listing of free items, visit OSHA's website at www.osha.gov or contact the OSHA Publications Office, U.S. Department of Labor, 200 Constitution Avenue, NW, N-3101, Washington, DC 20210; telephone (202) 693-1888 or fax to (202) 693-2498.

Contacting OSHA

To report an emergency, file a complaint, or seek OSHA advice, assistance, or products, call (800) 321-

OSHA or contact your nearest OSHA Regional office listed at the end of this publication. The teletypewriter (TTY) number is (877) 889-5627.

Written correspondence can be mailed to the nearest OSHA Regional or Area Office listed at the end of this publication or to OSHA's national office at: U.S. Department of Labor, Occupational Safety and Health Administration, 200 Constitution Avenue, N.W., Washington, DC 20210.

By visiting OSHA's website at www.osha.gov, you can also:

- File a complaint online,
- Submit general inquiries about workplace safety and health electronically, and
- Find more information about OSHA and occupational safety and health.

Occupational Safety and
Health Administration

OSHA Regional Offices

Region I
(CT,* ME, MA, NH, RI, VT*)
JFK Federal Building, Room E340
Boston, MA 02203
(617) 565-9860

Region II
(NJ,* NY,* PR,* VI*)
201 Varick Street, Room 670
New York, NY 10014
(212) 337-2378

Region III
(DE, DC, MD,* PA, VA,* WV)
The Curtis Center
170 S. Independence Mall West
Suite 740 West
Philadelphia, PA 19106-3309
(215) 861-4900

Region IV
(AL, FL, GA, KY,* MS, NC,* SC,* TN*)
61 Forsyth Street, SW, Room 6T50
Atlanta, GA 30303
(404) 562-2300

Region V
(IL, IN,* MI,* MN,* OH, WI)
230 South Dearborn Street
Room 3244
Chicago, IL 60604
(312) 353-2220

Region VI
(AR, LA, NM,* OK, TX)
525 Griffin Street, Room 602
Dallas, TX 75202
(972) 850-4145

Region VII
(IA,* KS, MO, NE)
Two Pershing Square
2300 Main Street, Suite 1010
Kansas City, MO 64108-2416
(816) 283-8745

Region VIII
(CO, MT, NO, SO, UT,* WY*)
1999 Broadway, Suite 1690
PO Box 46550
Denver, CO 80202-5716
(720) 264-6550

Region IX
(AZ,* CA,* HI,* NV,* and American Samoa,
Guam and the Northern Mariana Islands)
90 7th Street, Suite 18-100
San Francisco, CA 94103
(415) 625-2547

Region X
(AK,* ID, OR,* WA*)
1111 Third Avenue, Suite 715
Seattle, WA 98101-3212
(206) 553-5930

* These states and territories operate their own OSHA-approved job safety and health programs and cover state and local government employees as well as private sector employees. The Connecticut, New Jersey, New York and Virgin Islands plans cover public employees only. States with approved programs must have standards that are identical to, or at least as effective as, the Federal OSHA standards.

Note: To get contact information for OSHA Area Offices, OSHA-approved State Plans and OSHA Consultation Projects, please visit us online at www.osha.gov or call us at 1-800-321-0SHA.

(OOC 02/2009)

www.ingramcontent.com/pod-product-compliance
Lightning Source LLC
Chambersburg PA
CBHW081751170526
45167CB00009B/4000